AMARU

TUPAC
RESURRECTION
1971–1996

Original concept by Afeni Shakur
Edited by Jacob Hoye and Karolyn Ali
Photo Editor: Walter Einenkel
Based on the Film Directed by Lauren Lazin

ATRIA BOOKS
New York London Toronto Sydney

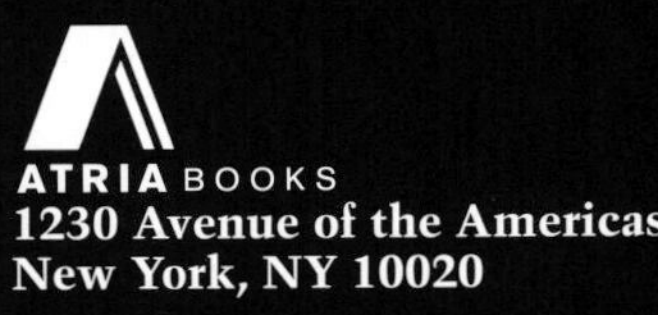

1230 Avenue of the Americas
New York, NY 10020

For information, address Atria Books, 1230 Avenue of the Americas, New York, NY 10020

ISBN-13: 978-0-7434-7434-4
ISBN-10: 0-7434-7434-1
ISBN-13: 978-0-7434-7435-1 (Pbk)
ISBN-10: 0-7434-7435-X (Pbk)

First Atria Books trade paperback edition March 2006

10 9 8 7 6 5 4 3 2 1

Manufactured in the United States of America

For information regarding special discounts for bulk purchases, please contact Simon & Schuster Special Sales at 1-800-456-6798 or business@simonandschuster.com

Photo credits can be found on page 251.

MAMA RAISED A HELLRAZOR

1 Born Thuggin Heartless & Mean mugging
AT 16 on the Scene watching FIENDS Bugging
2 Kicking up DUST with the older G
Soaking up the Game that was told to me
3 Never touched a GAT that I couldn't Shoot
Learn not 2 Trust a Bitch From the prostitutes
4 When Taught lessons 4 young Nigga asking questionz
while other suckas was guessing I was gangsta sex in
~~Elementary I was meant 2 be~~
5 Elementary it wasn't meant 4 me
can't regret it Headed 4 the Pentitiary and
6 cutting classing I buck buck blast straight moshing
mobbing thru the overpass laughing
7 while other motherfuckas try 2 figure out
NO Doubt they Jealous of Niggaz clout
8 Tell me Lord can ya Feel me
~~got a brotha riding with a strap cuz some niggaz tryin 2 kill me~~
I Keep my Finga on the trigga cuz some niggaz tryn 2 kill me
9 MAMA raised a Hellrazor
Every day getting paid police on my Pager
10 Straight Stressing a fugitive my occupation
is under question I'm Wanted 4 investigation
11 & All the while getting high
~~Pussy ass cops Don't Worry me bury me a G~~
12 Even though I'm Marked 4 Death
I'll spark til I loose my Breath
13 Everytime I read the Paper I C my Picture
When a nigga get Richer they come 2 get
14 it's All like a Motherfucking trap
& they wonda why it's hard being Black

NEW YORK
1971–1984

EVERYBODY'S PAST IS WHAT MADE THEIR FUTURE. IT'S ABOUT DESTINY.

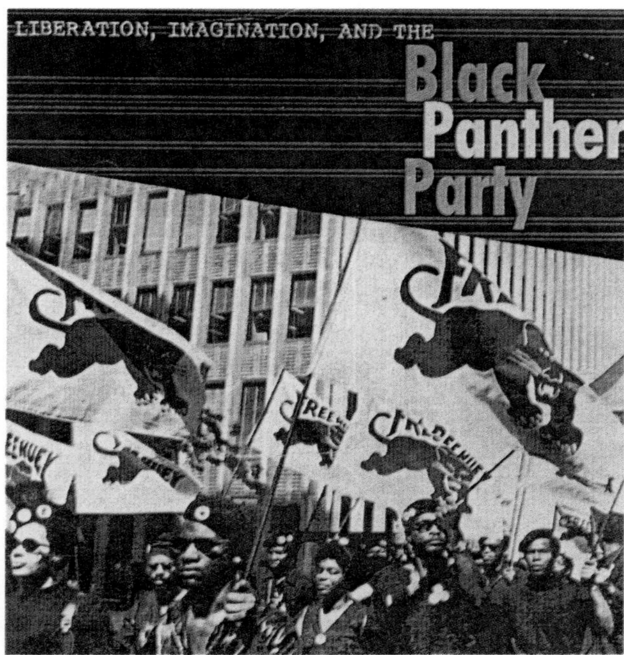
LIBERATION, IMAGINATION, AND THE
Black
Panther
Party

MY MOTHER WAS A BLACK PANTHER AND SHE WAS REALLY INVOLVED IN THE MOVEMENT.

Just black people bettering themselves and things like that. She was in a high position in the party which was unheard of because there was sexism, even in the Panthers. All my roots to the struggle are real deep. My stepfather at the time, Mutulu Shakur, he was also a well-known revolutionary. And then my godfather, Geronimo Pratt, he had a top official rank position with the Panthers on the West Coast.

There's racism, so when the Panthers hit, the government panicked and they felt like the Panthers were detrimental to American society. So they raided every Panthers' house, especially the ones who they felt like, could do damage as an orator. My mother was seven months pregnant, they put a match to the door and said "Fire, Fire!" And you know it's like five in the morning so my mother opened the door and they just burst in, put a shotgun to her pregnant belly and put a gun to her head and said, "Don't move, bah, bah, bah, you're under arrest." They treated them like less than humans.

MY MOTHER WAS PREGNANT WITH ME WHILE SHE WAS IN PRISON. SHE WAS HER OWN ATTORNEY. NEVER BEEN TO LAW SCHOOL. SHE WAS FACING THREE-HUNDRED-SOME ODD YEARS. ONE BLACK WOMAN, PREGNANT, BEAT THE CASE. THAT JUST GOES TO SHOW YOU THE STRENGTH OF A BLACK WOMAN AND THE STRENGTH OF THE OPPRESSED.

A month after she got outta prison she gave birth to me. So I was cultivated in prison, my embryo was in prison.

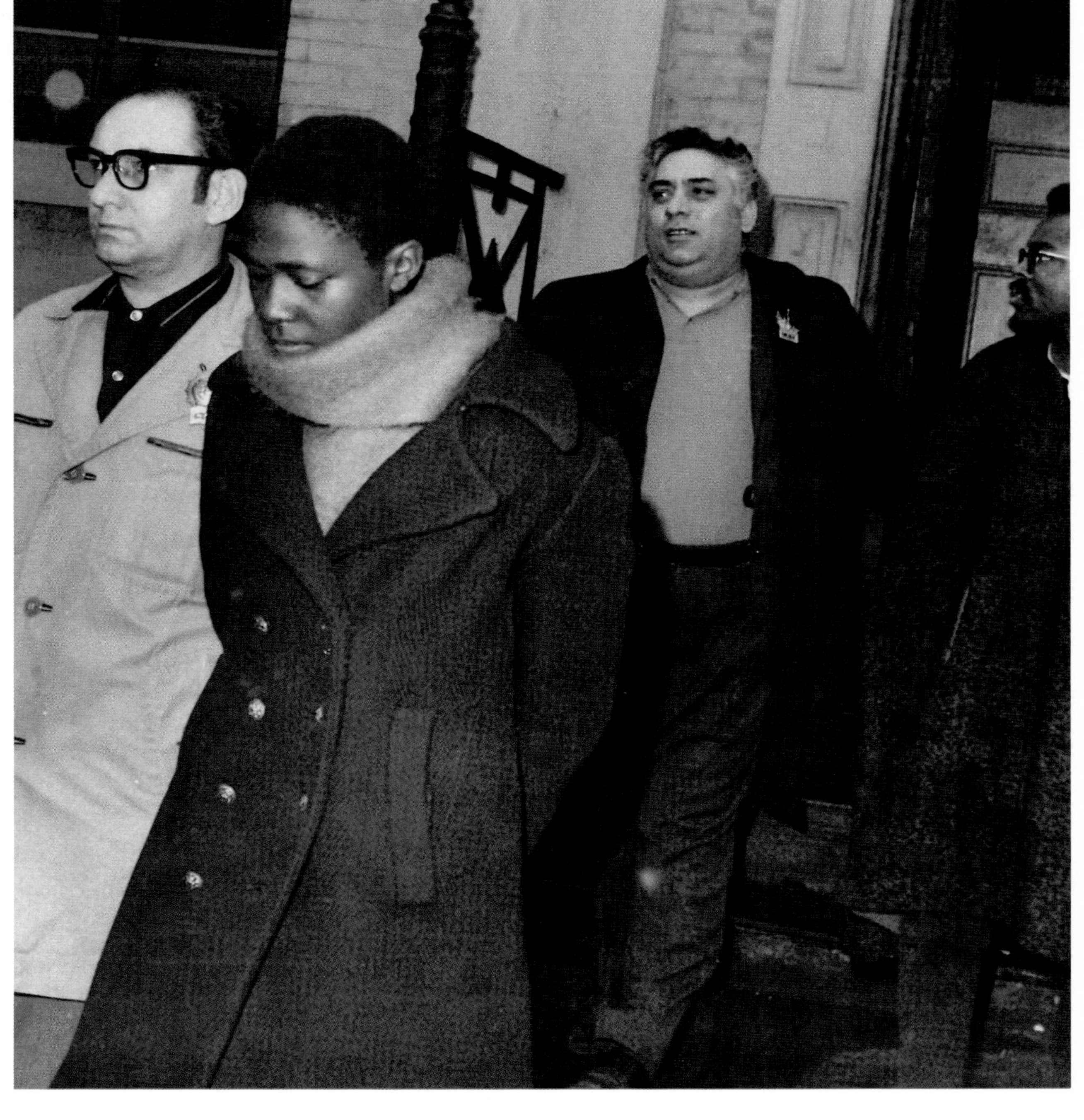

WHEN I WAS A BABY I REMEMBER ONE MOMENT OF CALM PEACE, THEN THREE MINUTES AFTER THAT IT WAS ON. I WAS NAMED AFTER THIS INCA CHIEF FROM SOUTH AMERICA WHOSE NAME WAS TUPAC AMARU. I THINK THE TRIBAL BREAK-DOWN MEANS "INTELLIGENT WARRIOR." HE'S A DEEP DUDE. IF I GO TO SOUTH AMERICA THEY GONNA LOVE ME, I'M TELLING YOU. THEY KNOW TUPAC.

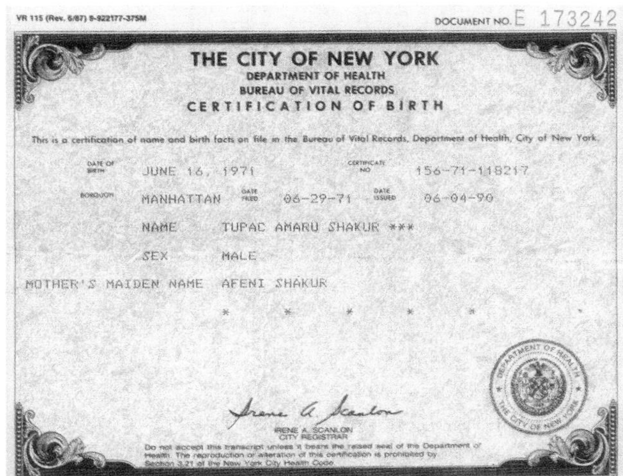

VR 115 (Rev. 6/87) 9-922177-375M DOCUMENT NO. E 173242

THE CITY OF NEW YORK
DEPARTMENT OF HEALTH
BUREAU OF VITAL RECORDS
CERTIFICATION OF BIRTH

This is a certification of name and birth facts on file in the Bureau of Vital Records, Department of Health, City of New York.

DATE OF BIRTH JUNE 16, 1971 CERTIFICATE NO 156-71-118217

BOROUGH MANHATTAN DATE FILED 06-29-71 DATE ISSUED 06-04-90

NAME TUPAC AMARU SHAKUR ***

SEX MALE

MOTHER'S MAIDEN NAME AFENI SHAKUR

* * * * *

Irene A. Scanlon
IRENE A. SCANLON
CITY REGISTRAR

Do not accept this transcript unless it bears the raised seal of the Department of Health. The reproduction or alteration of this certification is prohibited by Section 3.21 of the New York City Health Code.

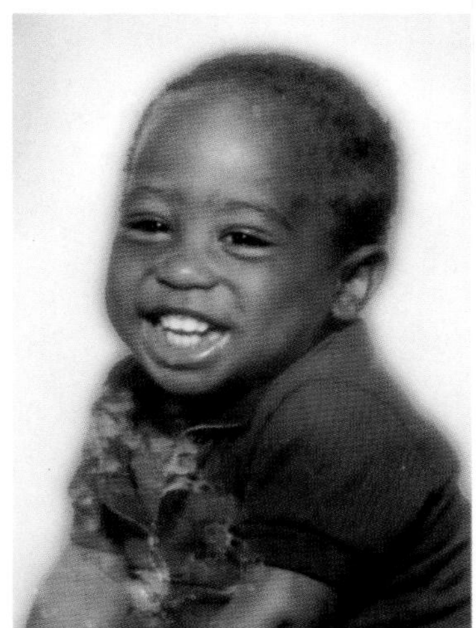

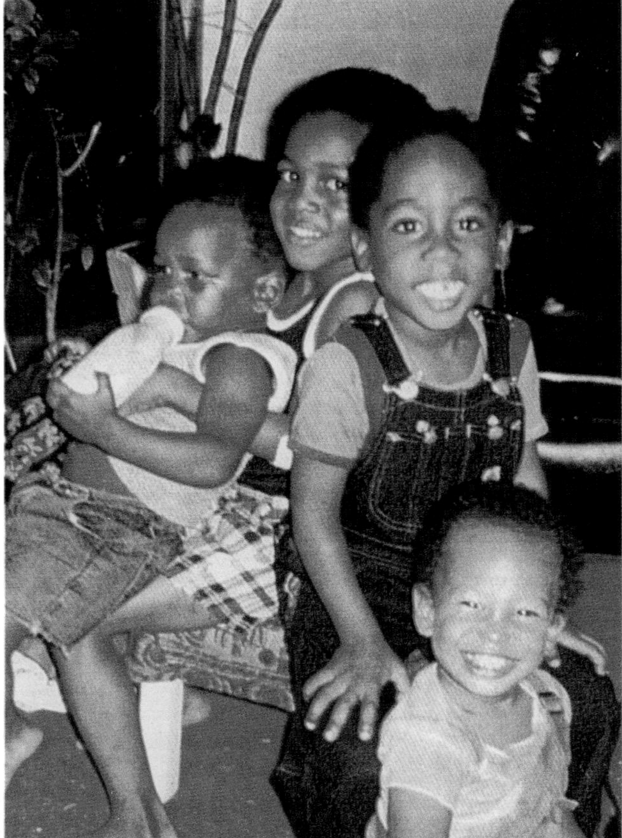

MY MOM IS THE BOMB.

First I rebelled against her because she was in the movement and we never spent time together because she was always speaking and going to colleges and everything. I always used to feel that she cared about "the" people more than "her" people. And then, after that was over, it was more time spent with me and we were both just like, "You're my mother?" And she's like, "You're my son." So then she was really close with me and really strict almost.

She taught me how to be community orientated. And I think my mother taught me how to understand women a lot more than my peers can. I'm not uncomfortable around strong women. My sister is the bomb too. She's my biggest critic, she's real smart, funny as all hell.

I THINK THAT MY MOTHER, LIKE FRED HAMPTON, MARK CLARK, HARRIET TUBMAN, THEY FELT LIKE THEY WERE LAYING TRACKS FOR THE GENERATION TO COME. SOMEBODY HAS TO BREAK OUT AND RISK LOSING EVERYTHING AND BEING POOR AND GETTING BEAT DOWN; SOMEBODY SACRIFICES.

But poverty, it's no joke. If there was no money and everything depended on your moral standards and the way you treated people, we'd be millionaires, we'd be rich. But since it's not like that, we're stone broke. And that's the only thing I'm bitter about is, growing up poor because I missed out on a lot of things. I can't always have what I want or even things that I think I need. I feel that my mother made a lot of decisions in her life—she could have chose to go to college and been well off. But she chose to fight and make things better.

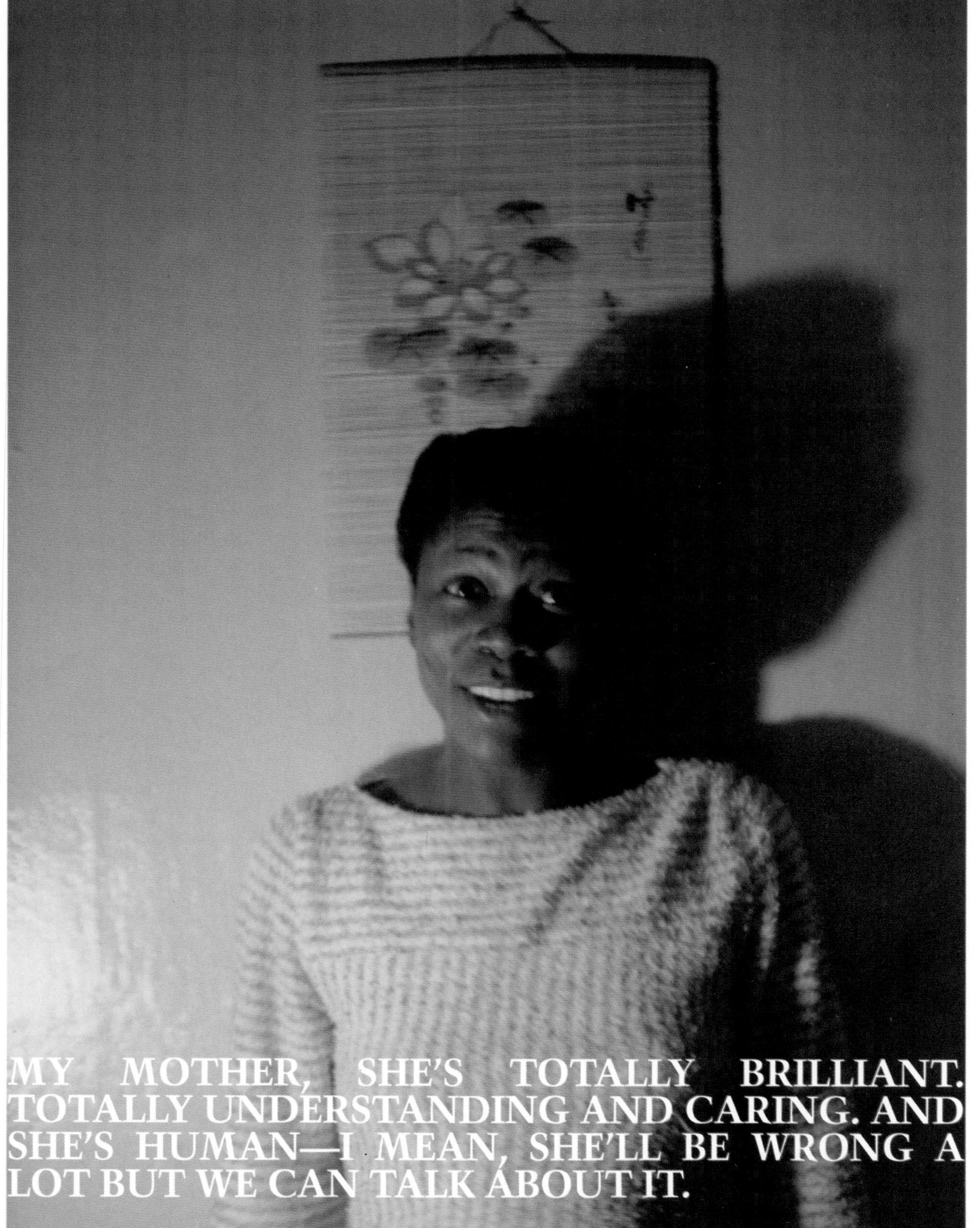
MY MOTHER, SHE'S TOTALLY BRILLIANT. TOTALLY UNDERSTANDING AND CARING. AND SHE'S HUMAN—I MEAN, SHE'LL BE WRONG A LOT BUT WE CAN TALK ABOUT IT.

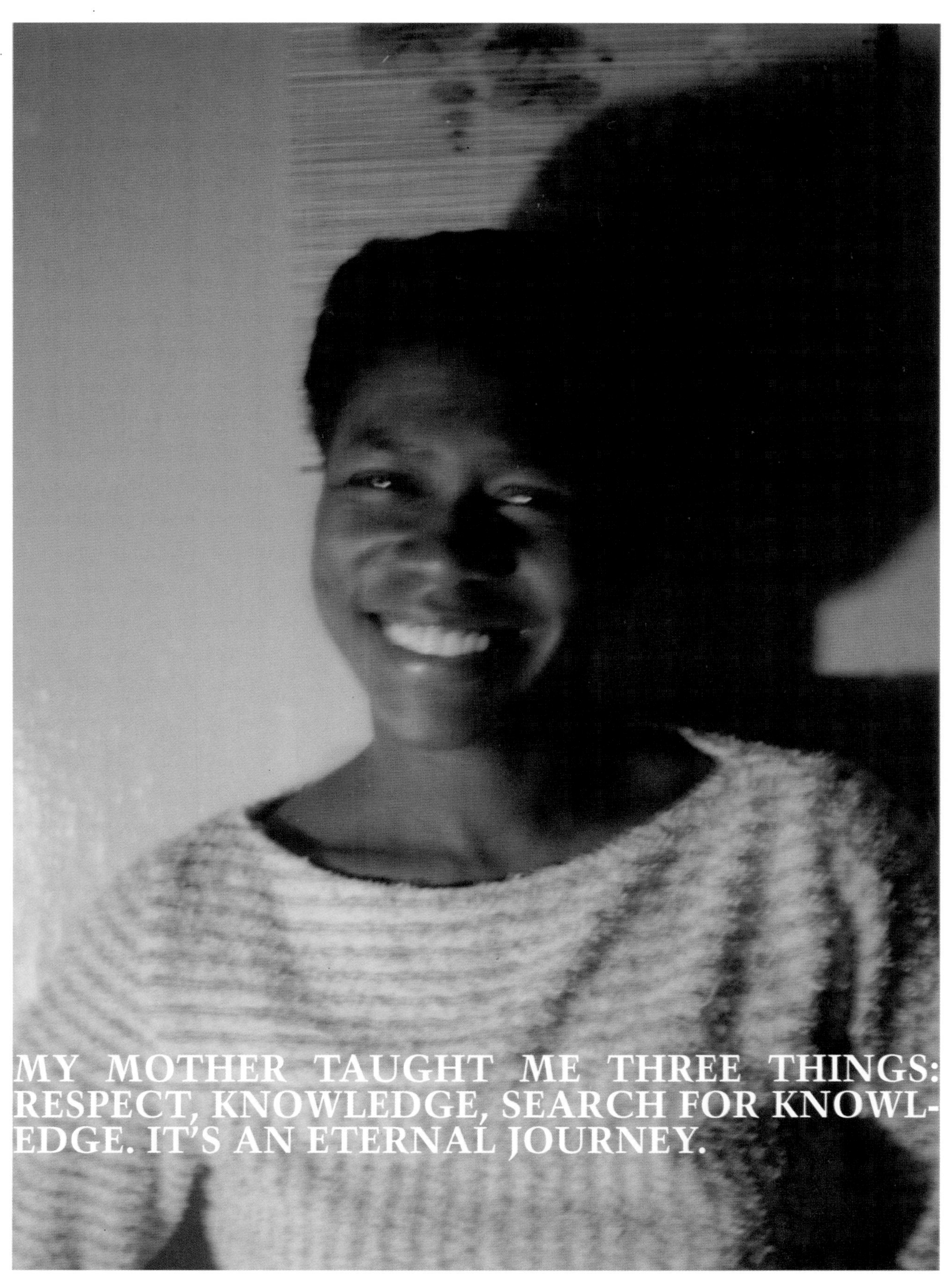
MY MOTHER TAUGHT ME THREE THINGS: RESPECT, KNOWLEDGE, SEARCH FOR KNOWL-EDGE. IT'S AN ETERNAL JOURNEY.

SHE ALWAYS TELLS ME THAT THE PAYOFF TO HER IS THAT ME AND MY SISTER GREW UP GOOD AND WE HAVE GOOD MINDS—BUT WE JUST DIDN'T HAVE MONEY.

POVERTY. IF I HATED ANYTHING, IT'D BE THAT.

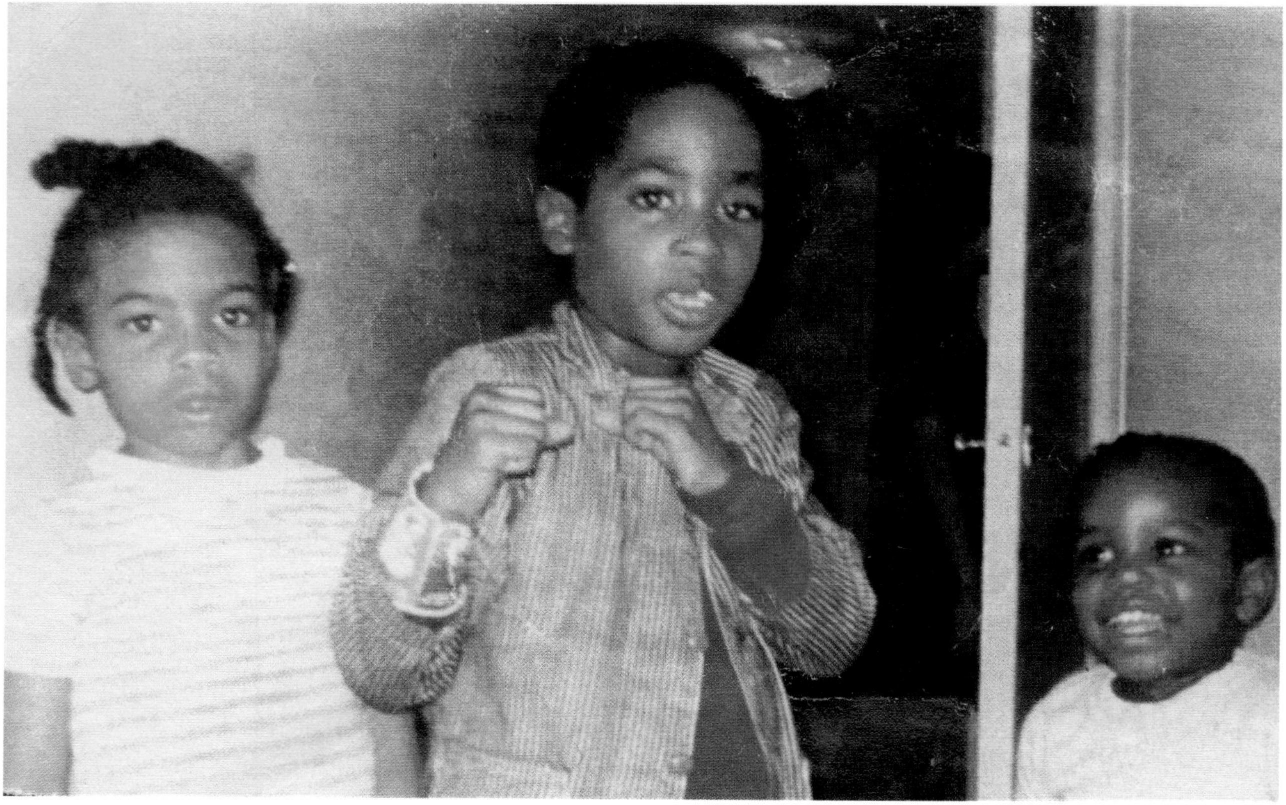

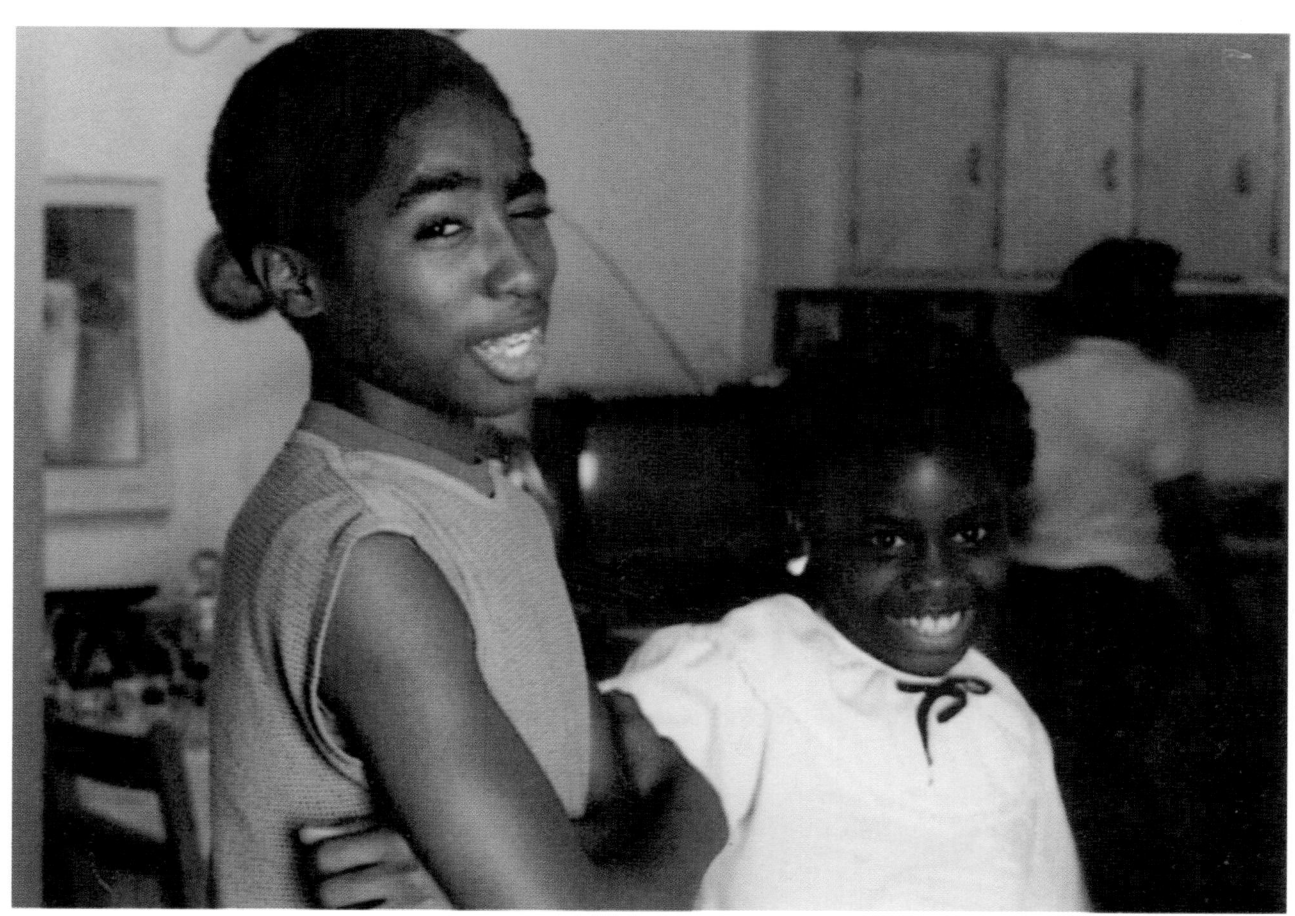

MY FATHER WAS A PANTHER.

I never knew where my father was or who my father was for sure. The times that I came up, it was the late sixties. They were still having free love, they was just hittin' what they was hittin'. My mother wasn't married, and she got pregnant and had me, and I didn't have a father.

MY STEPFATHER WAS A GANGSTA. A STRAIGHT-UP STREET HUSTLER. HE LOVED THE FACT THAT THE PANTHERS WOULD GO TO JAIL AND WOULDN'T SNITCH. HE DIDN'T EVEN CARE MY MOMS HAD A KID. HE WAS LIKE, "OH, THAT'S MY SON." TOOK CARE OF ME, GAVE ME MONEY, BUT HE WAS LIKE A CRIMINAL TOO. HE WAS A DRUG DEALER OUT THERE DOING HIS THING—HE ONLY CAME, BROUGHT ME MONEY, AND THEN LEFT.

I hate saying this cuz white people love hearing black people talking about this. But I know for a fact that had I had a father, I'd have some discipline. I'd have more confidence.

Your mother cannot calm you down the way a man can. Your mother can't reassure you the way a man can. My mother couldn't show me where my manhood was. You need a man to teach you how to be a man.

When I was young I was quiet, withdrawn. I read a lot, wrote poetry, kept a diary. I watched TV all day. I stayed in front of the television.

It was when I was in front of the TV by myself, being alone in the house by myself, having to cook dinner by myself, eat by myself. Just being by myself and looking at TV, at families and all these people out there in this pretend world. I knew I could be part of it if I pretended too, so early on I just watched and emulated . . . and I just thirsted for that. I thought if I could be and act like those characters, act like those people, I could have some of their joy. If I could act like I had a big family I wouldn't feel as lonely.

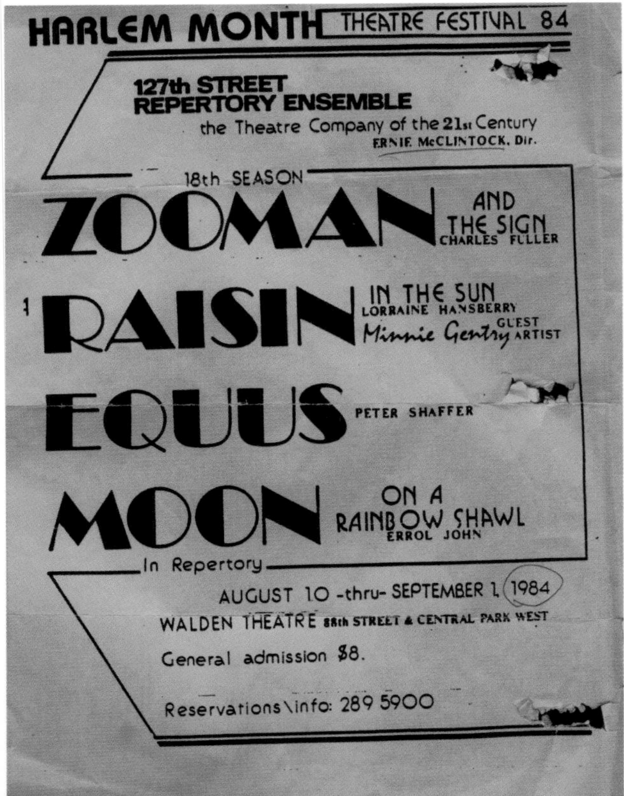

HARLEM MONTH THEATRE FESTIVAL 84

127th STREET REPERTORY ENSEMBLE

the Theatre Company of the 21st Century

ERNIE McCLINTOCK, Dir.

18th SEASON

ZOOMAN AND THE SIGN
CHARLES FULLER

RAISIN IN THE SUN
LORRAINE HANSBERRY
Minnie Gentry GUEST ARTIST

EQUUS
PETER SHAFFER

MOON ON A RAINBOW SHAWL
ERROL JOHN

In Repertory

AUGUST 10 -thru- SEPTEMBER 1, 1984

WALDEN THEATRE 88th STREET & CENTRAL PARK WEST

General admission $8.

Reservations\info: 289 5900

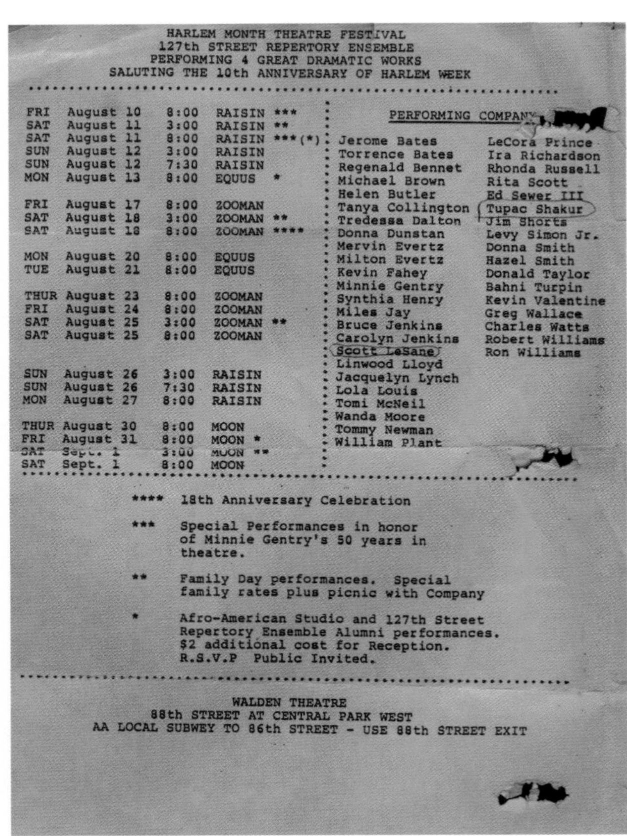

HARLEM MONTH THEATRE FESTIVAL
127th STREET REPERTORY ENSEMBLE
PERFORMING 4 GREAT DRAMATIC WORKS
SALUTING THE 10th ANNIVERSARY OF HARLEM WEEK

FRI	August 10	8:00	RAISIN ***
SAT	August 11	3:00	RAISIN **
SAT	August 11	8:00	RAISIN ***(*)
SUN	August 12	3:00	RAISIN
SUN	August 12	7:30	RAISIN
MON	August 13	8:00	EQUUS *
FRI	August 17	8:00	ZOOMAN
SAT	August 18	3:00	ZOOMAN **
SAT	August 18	8:00	ZOOMAN ****
MON	August 20	8:00	EQUUS
TUE	August 21	8:00	EQUUS
THUR	August 23	8:00	ZOOMAN
FRI	August 24	8:00	ZOOMAN
SAT	August 25	3:00	ZOOMAN **
SAT	August 25	8:00	ZOOMAN
SUN	August 26	3:00	RAISIN
SUN	August 26	7:30	RAISIN
MON	August 27	8:00	RAISIN
THUR	August 30	8:00	MOON
FRI	August 31	8:00	MOON *
SAT	Sept. 1	3:00	MOON **
SAT	Sept. 1	8:00	MOON

PERFORMING COMPANY

Jerome Bates
Torrence Bates
Regenald Bennet
Michael Brown
Helen Butler
Tanya Collington
Tredessa Dalton
Donna Dunstan
Mervin Evertz
Milton Evertz
Kevin Fahey
Minnie Gentry
Synthia Henry
Miles Jay
Bruce Jenkins
Carolyn Jenkins
Scott LeSane
Linwood Lloyd
Jacquelyn Lynch
Lola Louis
Tomi McNeil
Wanda Moore
Tommy Newman
William Plant
LeCora Prince
Ira Richardson
Rhonda Russell
Rita Scott
Ed Sewer III
Tupac Shakur
Jim Shorts
Levy Simon Jr.
Donna Smith
Hazel Smith
Donald Taylor
Bahni Turpin
Kevin Valentine
Greg Wallace
Charles Watts
Robert Williams
Ron Williams

**** 18th Anniversary Celebration

*** Special Performances in honor of Minnie Gentry's 50 years in theatre.

** Family Day performances. Special family rates plus picnic with Company

* Afro-American Studio and 127th Street Repertory Ensemble Alumni performances. $2 additional cost for Reception. R.S.V.P Public Invited.

WALDEN THEATRE
88th STREET AT CENTRAL PARK WEST
AA LOCAL SUBWEY TO 86th STREET - USE 88th STREET EXIT

A River That Flows Forever

4 mother

As long as some suffer
The River Flows Forever
As long as there is pain
The River Flows Forever
As strong as a smile can be
The River will Flow Forever
And as long as u R with me
we'll ride the River Together

BALTIMORE 1984–1988

THIS IS WHERE WE CHOSE TO LIVE.

BALTIMORE HAS THE HIGHEST RATE OF TEEN PREGNANCY, THE HIGHEST RATE OF AIDS WITHIN THE BLACK COMMUNITY, THE HIGHEST RATE OF TEENS KILLING TEENS, THE HIGHEST RATE OF TEEN SUICIDE, AND THE HIGHEST RATE OF BLACKS KILLING BLACKS. IN BALTIMORE, MARYLAND. AND THIS IS WHERE WE CHOSE TO LIVE.

GUCCI
GUCCI

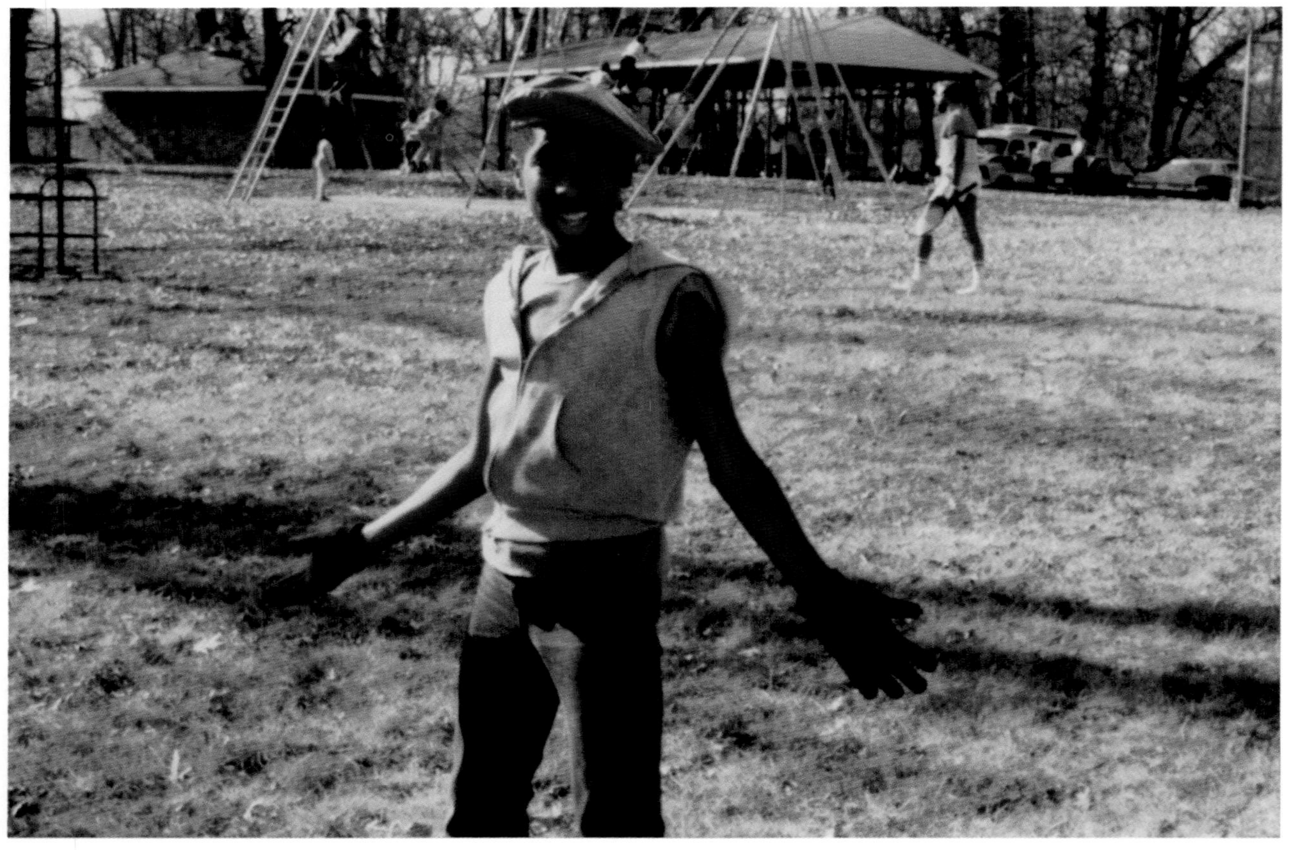

WE MOVED OUT TO NEW YORK BECAUSE MY MOTHER LOST HER JOB AND WE WERE LIKE STRANDED.

AND WE MOVED TO BALTIMORE WHICH WAS TOTAL IGNORANCE TOWN TO ME. IT GETS ME UPSET TO TALK ABOUT IT.

I HAD A FEW TIMES WHEN I JUST ZONED OUT AND HAD GOOD LUCK. WHEN I AUDITIONED FOR THE BALTIMORE SCHOOL FOR THE ARTS, THAT WAS ONE OF MY GOOD LUCK TIMES. I SPENT THREE YEARS IN BALTIMORE, MY HIGH SCHOOL YEARS. I LOVED MY CLASSES, MADE A LOT OF FRIENDS THAT I WANTED TO KEEP OVER.

WE WERE EXPOSED TO EVERYTHING.THEATER, BALLET, DIFFERENT PEOPLE'S LIFESTYLES—RICH PEOPLE'S LIFESTYLES, ROYALTY FROM OTHER COUNTRIES AND THINGS, EVERYTHING.

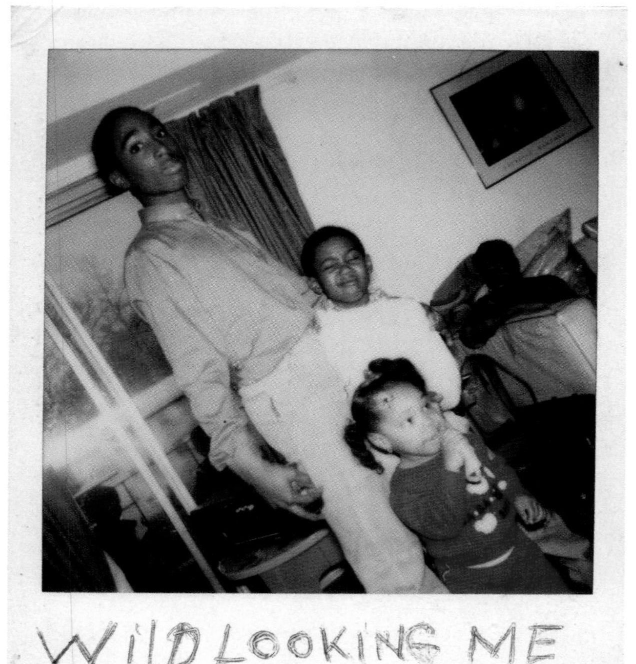

WildLOOKING ME
With KAHLIL + Quiana

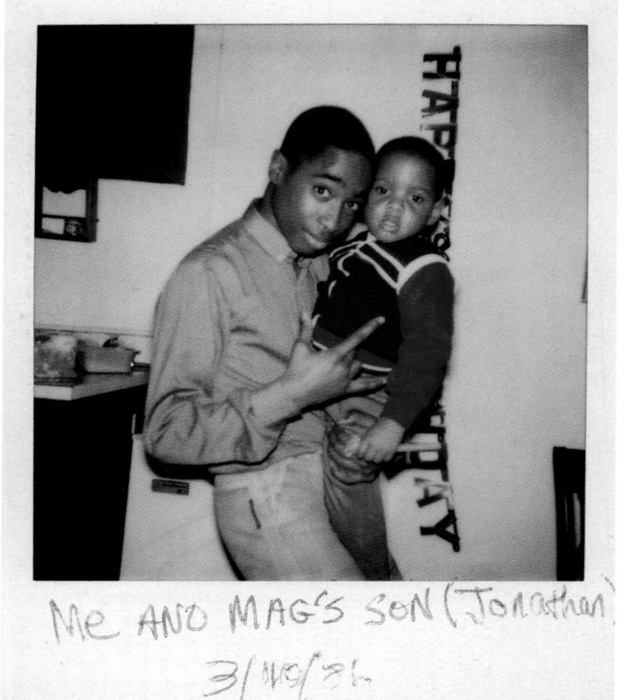

Me AND MAG'S SON (Jonathan)
3/10/86

4 JADA

u R THE omega of my Heart
THE foundation 4 my conception of Love
when I THINK of what a Black woman should be
it's u that I FIRST Think OF

u will never fully understand
How Deeply my Heart Feels 4 u
I worry that we'll grow apart
and I'll end up losing u

u Bring me 2 climax without sex
and u do it all with regal grace
u R my Heart in Human Form
a Friend I could never replace

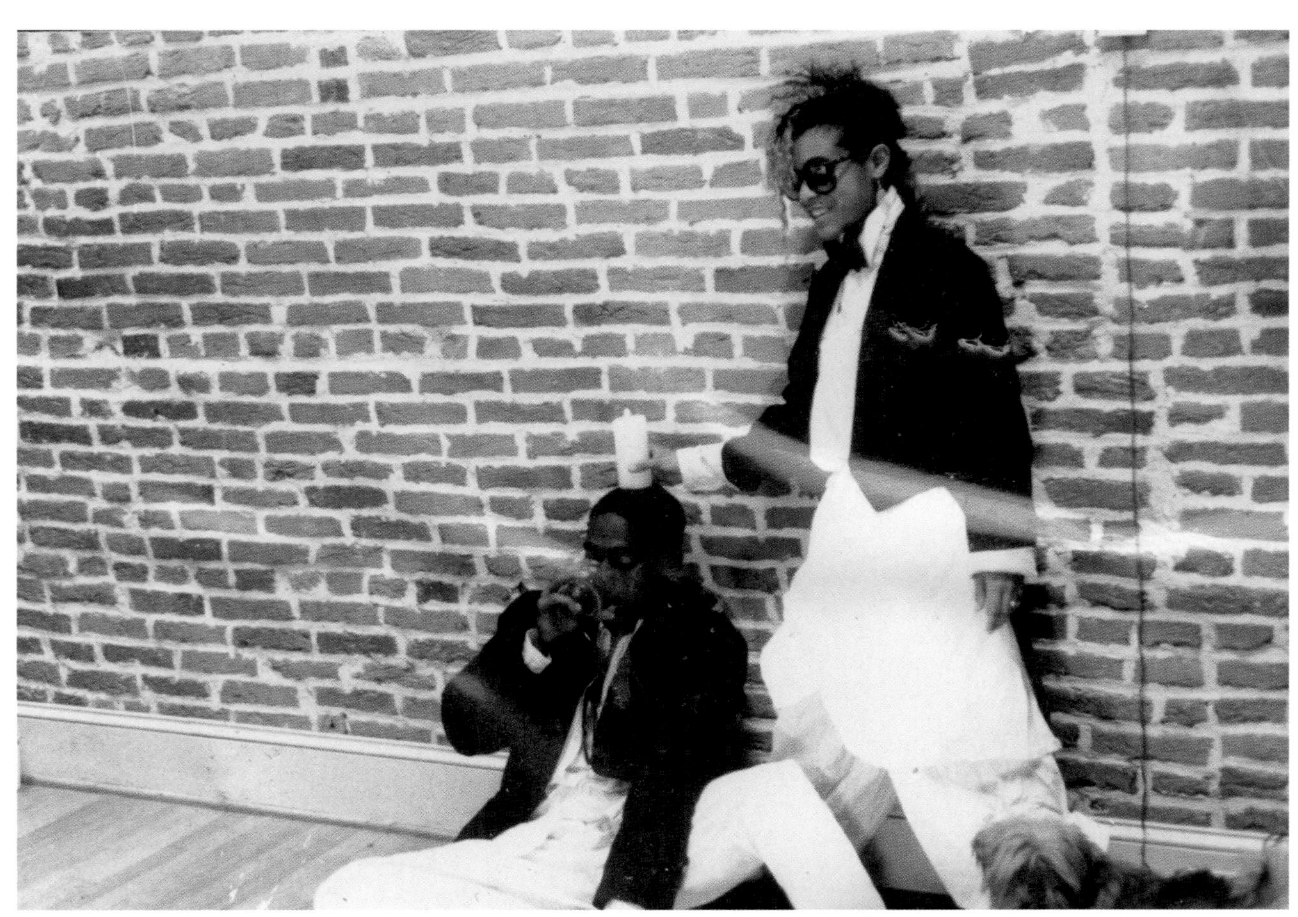

NOTHING CAN COME BETWEEN US
4 JOHN

let's not talk of money
let us forget the world
4 a moment let's just revel
in our eternal comradery
in my Heart I know
there will never be a day
that I don't remember
the times we shared
u were a friend
when I was at my lowest
and being a friend 2 me
was not easy nor fashionable
Regardless of how popular
I become u remain
my unconditional friend
unconditional in it's truest sense
Did u think I would forget
Did u 4 one moment dream
that I would ignore u
if so Remembee this from here 2 forever
nothing Can Come between us

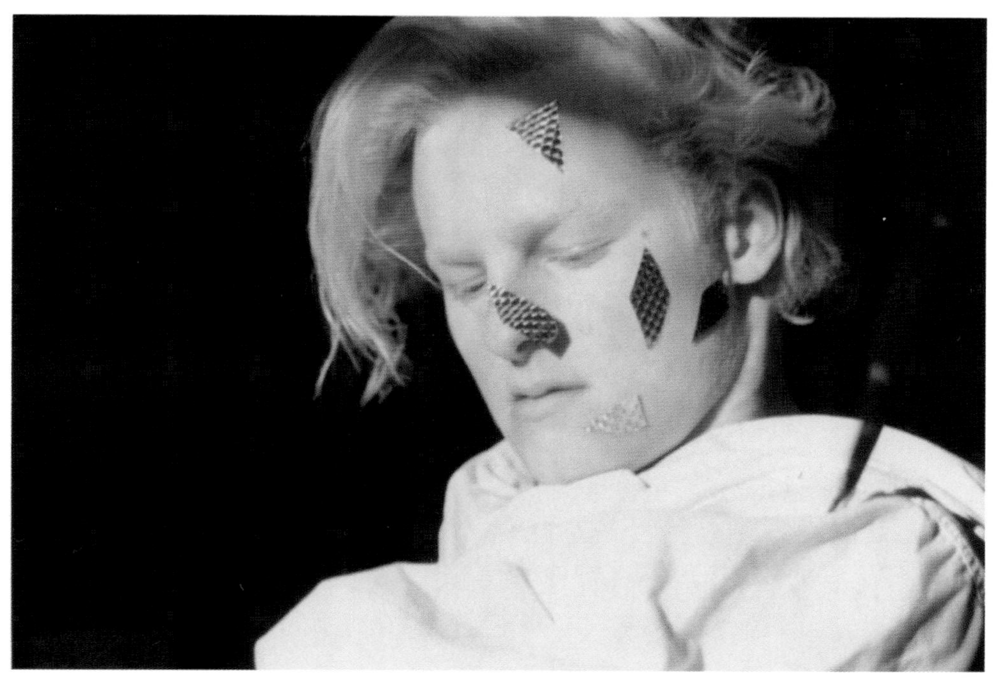

But at my homeboy's high school, it's not like that. They don't have trips to go see Broadway plays, they don't read the things we were reading, and they didn't know what I was talking about when I was like, "Yo, Shakespeare's dope." They don't have the same experiences that we had. Then I started thinking, like, damn, why is that? Cuz our school that I went to is mostly for white kids and rich minorities.

And I started going, Damn, man, I would have been a totally different person had I not been exposed to these things. Hell no, I was living in the ghetto. We didn't have any lights, no electricity. We was about to get evicted.

I thought, we're not being taught to deal with the world as it is. We're being taught to deal with this fairy tale land we're not even living in anymore. It's sad. I mean, more kids are being handed crack than they're being handed diplomas. I think adults should go through school again. I think rich people should live like poor people and poor people should live like rich people and they should change every week.

GROWING UP IN AMERICA—I LOVED MY CHILDHOOD BUT I HATED GROWING UP POOR, AND IT MADE ME VERY BITTER. WE LIVE IN HELL. WE LIVE IN THE GUTTER, A WAR ZONE.

They got us stacked up eighty deep in one building. By the time you get out of your house you strap just to protect yourself.

The same crime element that white people are scared of, black people are scared of. The same crime element that white people fear, we fear. So we defend ourselves from the same crime element that they scared of, you know what I'm saying? So while they waiting for legislation to pass, and everything, we next door to the killer. We next door to him cuz we up in the projects with eighty niggaz in a building. All them killers that they letting out, they right there in that building. But it's better? Just cuz we're black we get along with the killers or something? We get along with the rapists cuz we black and we from the same hood? What is that? We need protection too.

Marlboro

Liberty Needs Glasses

excuse me But lady liberty needs glasses
AND So Does mrs Justice By her side
Both the Broads R BlinD as Bats
Stumbling Thru' the system
Justice Bumbed into Mutulu and
Trippen on Geronimo Pratt
But stepped right over oliver
AND his crooked partner Ronnie
Justice stumbed her Big Toe on Mandela
AND liberty was misquoted By the indians
slavery was a learning phase
Forgotten with out a verdict
while Justice is on a rampage
4 endengered Surviving Black males
I mean Really if anyone really valued life
and cared about the masses
they'd take em Both 2 Pen optical
and get 2 pair of Glasses

she never got to make that trip so the Friends of the Fever
R going for her and every body else who couldn't make it.
We all worked hard and saved our money we hustled a lot
ran errands for the dealers they'd give big tips if u stayed
in School so we all went to School thru Max's beatings
and his hospital stay thru Rooster 6 month Visit
2 Juvie thru me & Square problems when the police we're
first really looking for my father. Thru all of that
we fantisized about the Exodus and finally
it was 2 be real. We were waiting Rooster 2 steal a
Car but nobody really wanted 2 go thru with the driving
us being so young & all and even if I did
look older it was a chance with all 5 of us
in the car so we took the train the
upstate link up with the Railroad cars that go
out west 2 california where we could all start
over together.

THEN I CAME TO CALIFORNIA TO ESCAPE THAT, ESCAPE THAT VIOLENCE.

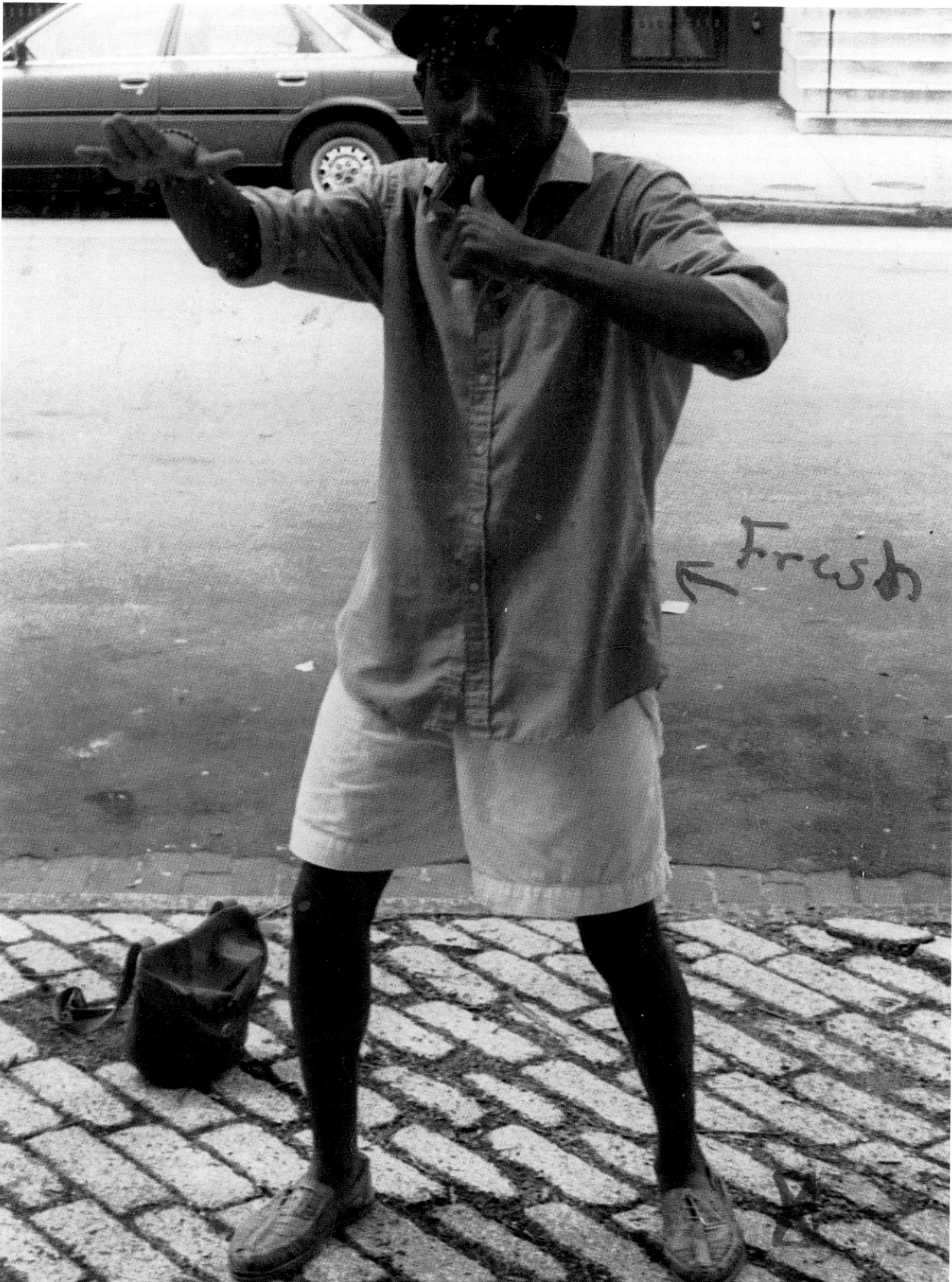
Fresh

OAKLAND 1988–1991

I KNOW GOOD THINGS ARE GONNA COME FOR ME.

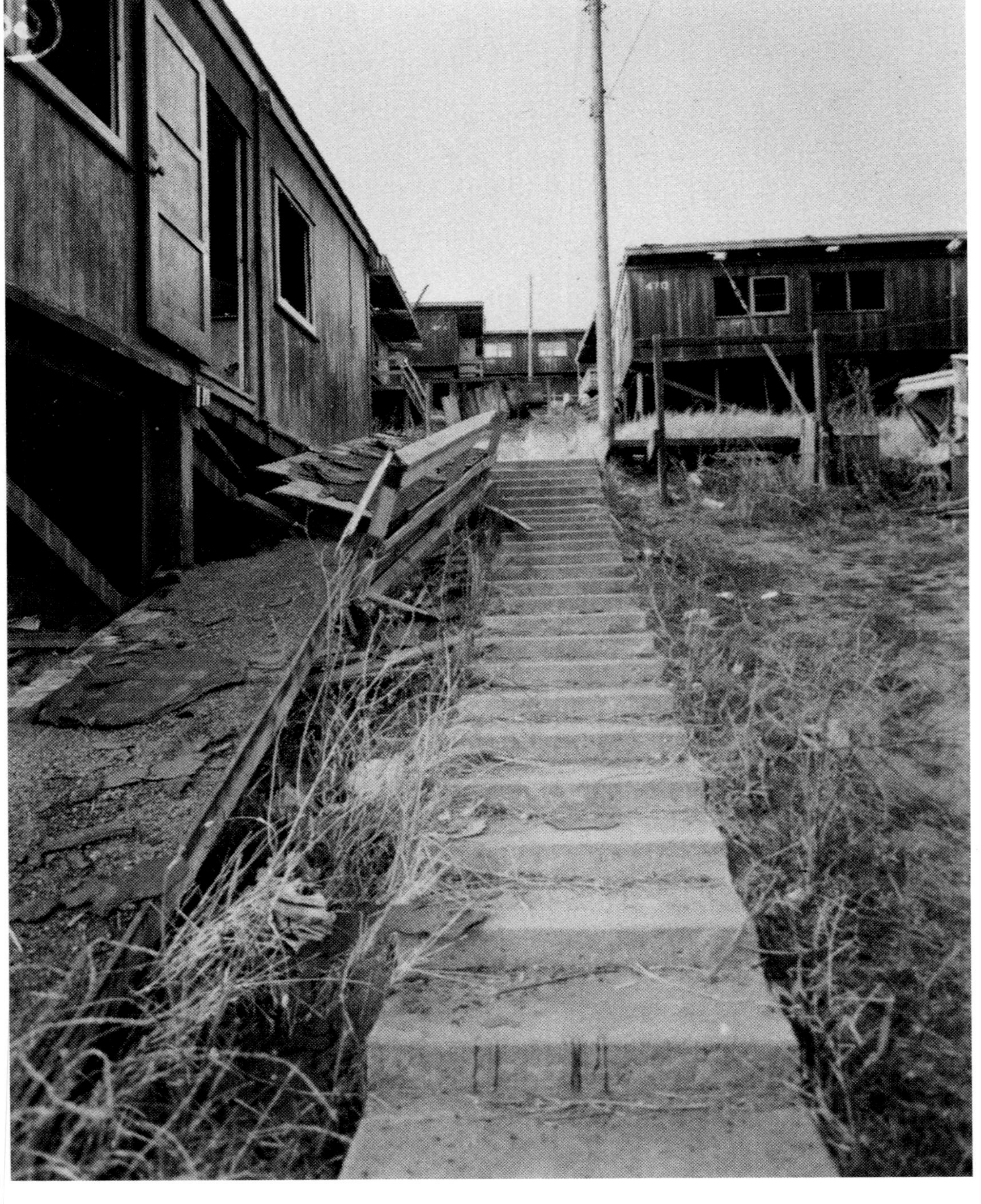

Come to Marin City and there's skinhead violence. There's racial violence, which I deplore. But don't get the wrong idea; I feel like I'm being gloomy. I don't mean to just be like, "Damn, it's bad out there." I still try to be positive.

I CHASE GIRLS AND WANT THE CAR AND LOUD MUSIC. BUT I LIKE TO THINK OF MYSELF AS SOCIALLY AWARE. I THINK THERE SHOULD BE A DRUG CLASS, A SEX EDUCATION CLASS. A REAL SEX EDUCATION CLASS. A CLASS ON POLICE BRUTALITY. THERE SHOULD BE A CLASS ON APARTHEID. THERE SHOULD BE A CLASS ON WHY PEOPLE ARE HUNGRY, BUT THERE ARE NOT. THERE ARE CLASSES ON . . . GYM. PHYSICAL EDUCATION. LET'S LEARN VOLLEYBALL.

LIFE THROUGH MY EYES

Life through my Bloodshot eyes
would scare a square 2 death
poverty, murder, violence
and never a moment 2 rest
fun and games R few
But treasured like gold 2 me
cuz I realize that I must return
2 my spot in poverty
But mock my words when I say
my heart will not exist
unless my destiny comes through
and puts and end 2 all of this

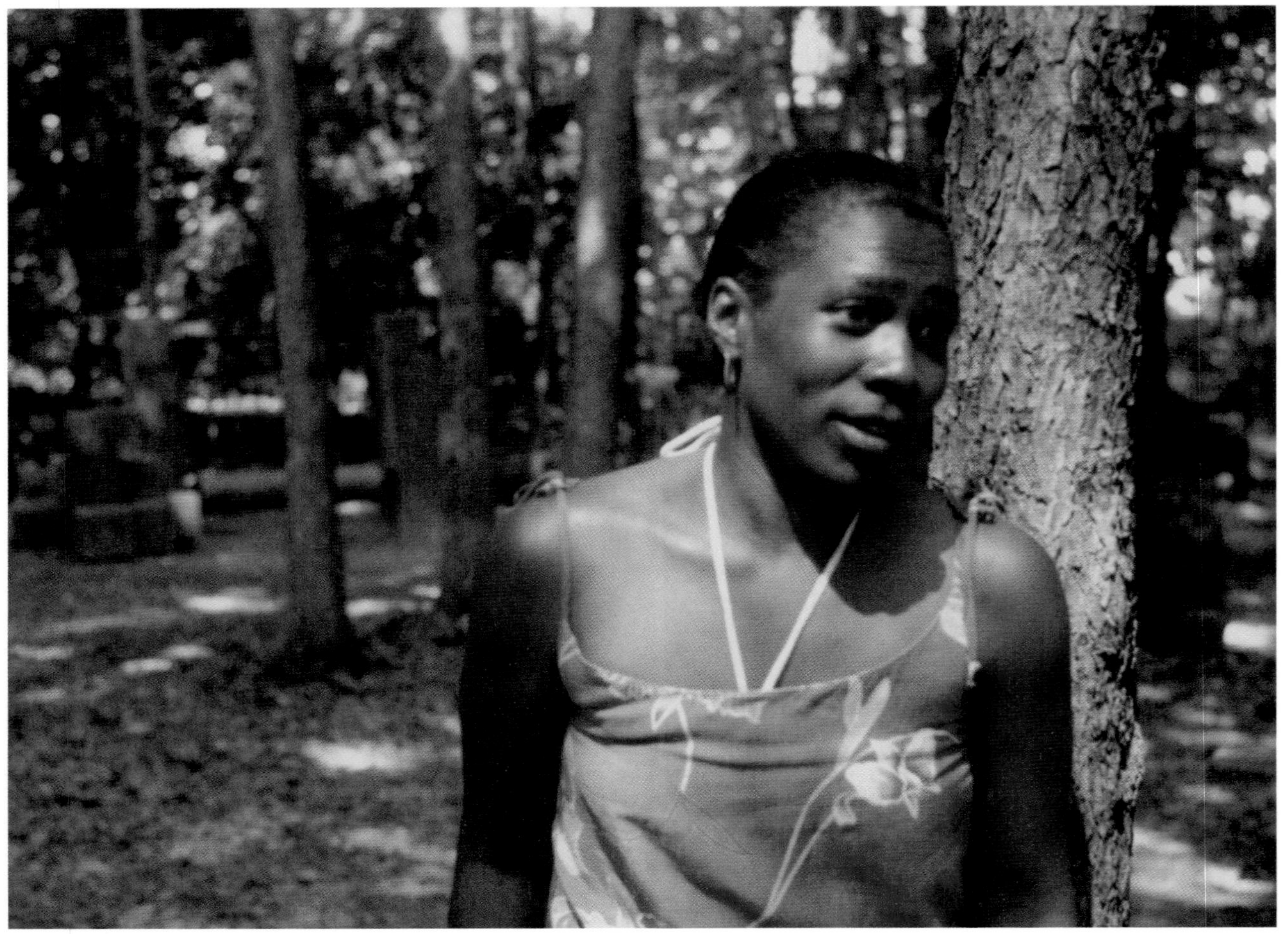

MY MOM'S MY HOMIE. WE WENT THROUGH OUR LITTLE . . . OUR STAGES, YOU KNOW, WHERE FIRST WE WAS MOTHER AND SON, THEN IT WAS LIKE DRILL SERGEANT AND CADET. THEN IT WAS DICTATOR, LITTLE COUNTRY. THEN I MOVED OUT, AND WAS ON MY OWN.

PANTHERS

I WAS BROKE, NOWHERE TO STAY. I SMOKED WEED. I HUNG OUT WITH THE DRUG DEALERS, PIMPS AND THE CRIMINALS. THEY WERE THE ONLY PEOPLE THAT CARED ABOUT ME AT THAT POINT. AND I NEEDED A FATHER—A MALE INFLUENCE IN MY LIFE, AND THESE WERE THE MALES.

My mom, she was lost at that particular moment. She wasn't caring about herself. She was addicted to crack. It was a hard time, because she was my hero.

I was broke. I didn't have enough credits to graduate. I dropped out. I said, "I gotta get paid, I gotta find a way to make a living."

I TRIED SELLING DRUGS FOR MAYBE LIKE TWO WEEKS. AND THEN THE DUDE WAS LIKE, "OH MAN, GIVE ME MY DRUGS BACK," CUZ I DIDN'T KNOW HOW TO DO IT. THEN THE DOPE DEALERS USED TO LOOK OUT FOR ME. THEY WOULD JUST GIVE ME MONEY AND BE LIKE, "DON'T GET INVOLVED IN THIS. GET OUT THERE AND DO YOUR DREAM." SO THEY WERE LIKE MY SPONSORS.

ALL MY SONGS DEAL WITH PAIN. THAT'S WHAT MAKES ME *ME,* THAT'S WHAT MAKES ME DO WHAT I DO. EVERYTHING IS BASED ON THE PAIN I FELT IN MY CHILDHOOD. SMALL PIECES OF IT AND HARSH PIECES OF IT.

My inspiration for writing music is like Don McLean did when he did "American Pie" or "Vincent." Lorraine Hansberry with *A Raisin in the Sun.* Like Shakespeare when he does his thing, like deep stories, like raw human needs.

I'm trying to think of a good analogy. It's like, you've got the Vietnam War, and because you had reporters showing us pictures of the war at home, that's what made the war end, or that shit would have lasted longer. If no one knew what was going on we would have thought they were just dying valiantly in some beautiful way. But because we saw the horror, that's what made us stop the war.

SO I THOUGHT, THAT'S WHAT I'M GOING TO DO AS AN ARTIST, AS A RAPPER. I'M GONNA SHOW THE MOST GRAPHIC DETAILS OF WHAT I SEE IN MY COMMUNITY AND HOPEFULLY THEY'LL STOP IT QUICK.

I'VE SEEN ALL OF THAT—THE CRACK BABIES, WHAT WE HAD TO GO THROUGH, LOSING EVERYTHING, BEING POOR, AND GETTING BEAT DOWN. ALL OF THAT. BEING THE PERSON I AM, I SAID NO NO NO NO. I'M CHANGING THIS.

The only WAY 2 change me is maybe blow my brains out
STUCK in the middle of the game can't get the Pain out
I Pray 2 my GOD everyday but he don't listen
the poverty bothers me but mama working Wondaz in the Kitchen
listen I can hear her crying in the Bedroom
Praying 4 money she'll never get will we be Dead Soon
Am I wrong 4 wishing I was somewhere else
13 can't feed myself can I
Blame Daddy cuz he left me wish he would've hug me
2 much like him so my mama don't love me
ON my own at an early age getting Paid
STAY STRAPPED so I'll never be afraid
where did I Go astray hanging in the backstreetz
running with Gz & dopefiends will they Jack me
CANT TURN Back my eyez on the Prize
I got nothing 2 lose cuz everybody gotta Die
Say Goodbye 2 the bad guy the 1 u fucked when u passby
B B from the Glock let the glass fly
Do or Die walk a mile in my shoez
& u'd be crazy 2

But when I first started rapping I needed the money and I had to work. The dance with the naked doll? That was me. For me to get paid I had to go out there in bikini briefs and hop on top of this doll. I was homeless at the time and that's what I had to do. You have to work from one point to get to another point. I admire the work ethic.

I USED TO RAP EVERYWHERE. I WAS ONE OF THOSE PEOPLE, I PUT MY TAPE IN THE DECK, I INTERRUPT CONVERSATIONS AND JUST START RAPPING.

This lady named Leila introduced me to Atron Gregory who was managing Digital Underground. He was like, "I'ma send you to Digital Underground, they in the studio. You just rap for Shock G on the spot. If he like you, I'ma pick you up."

I just walked in and rapped for him. He's like, "OK, good, you're in, boom-boom-boom, I'll see you later." I just walked out of there like, dang!

I look back with the greatest fondness. Those were like some of the best times in my life. It's all funny to me, it's all good. The silly part is like me running around in zebra print underwears, and making simulated sex. We had like the funniest, craziest show. I think hip-hop needs another Digital Underground right now.

Money B is the freaky deaky, you know? He adds that special sexy flavor for the females. Shock is the guru. He has a spiritual part. Humpty is the comic relief. Pee Wee is like that pimp, the gangsta sound. And I'm more the rebel. I speak for the young black males. I feel as though I can honestly say my ear is to the streets. Especially for the young black males in America in the ghettos, my ear is right there.

AS SOON AS I GOT A CHANCE TO SAY WHAT WAS ON MY MIND, I SAID WHAT WAS ON MY MIND AND WE HAVE A PLATINUM RECORD NOW. SO I WENT FROM DANCING NAKED WITH DOLLS, BEING UNKNOWN, TO HAVING A PLATINUM RECORD.

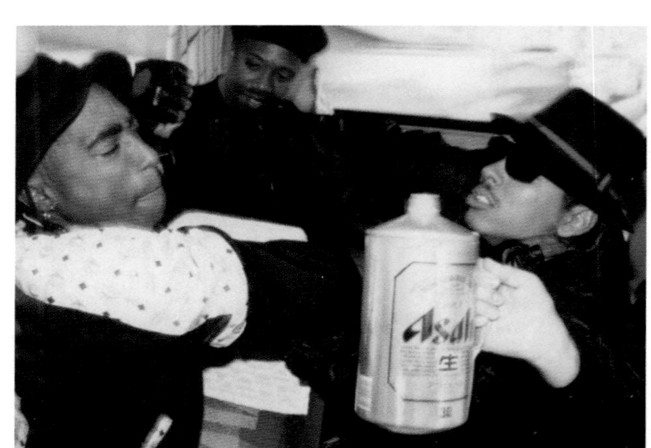
生

CLAIM AGAINST THE CITY OF OAKLAND, CALIFORNIA
CLAIMANT: TUPAC AMARU SHAKUR
Page One

TUPAC AMARU SHAKUR presents a claim for damages against the **City of Oakland, California, Dept. of Police, Chief of Police, GEORGE HART, Oakland Police Officers ALEXANDER BOYOVICH, KEVIN RODGERS, and DOES 1-25,** in the sum of **ten million dollars ($10,000,000.00)**

Claimant's Address: LAW OFFICES OF JOHN L. BURRIS, John L. Burris, 1212 Broadway, Suite 1200, Oakland, CA 94612

Address of party presenting claim, if other than above: LAW OFFICES OF JOHN L. BURRIS, John L. Burris, 1212 Broadway, Suite 1200, Oakland, CA 94612

Date of Occurrence: October 17, 1991

Place of Occurrence: In front of 1750 Broadway in the City of Oakland

Said claim arises from following circumstances:

On October 17, 1991, at approximately 12:45 p.m., Tupac (aka "2 Pac") Amaru Shakur ("claimant"), a young African American male and member of the nationally acclaimed "rap" group, Digital Underground, was physically and verbally assaulted, and falsely arrested and imprisoned by two Oakland Police officers, Alexander Boyovich and Kevin Rodgers, both white males.

At approximately 12:45 p.m., claimant jaywalked across

Broadway to enter Union Bank (the "Bank"). Officers Boyovich and Rodgers blocked claimant's entrance to the Bank and repeatedly requested his identification. Claimant complied with the officers' request and provided them with three (3) pieces of identification. Both officers immediately proceeded to joke and harass claimant about his name.

A discussion ensued regarding the issuance of the jaywalking ticket. At some point in the conversation, claimant informed the officers that he was a member of the "rap" group Digital Underground and merely wanted the ticket so that he could complete his banking business. Officer Boyovich immediately informed claimant that they could do whatever they desired to him, including arresting claimant for anything they wanted. Claimant informed the officers he had done nothing to warrant arrest. Uttering a profanity, claimant requested his citation.

At Claimant's request for his citation, Officer Boyovich responded by grabbing claimant by the neck, putting him in a choke hold and throwing him to the ground. As a result, claimant's face hit the sidewalk. While on the ground, Officer Boyovich repeatedly slammed claimant's face upon the pavement while Officer Rodgers held claimant's body down. Officer Boyovich continued to choke claimant until he loss consciousness. At no time did the claimant assault or resist the officers while they were physically attacking him.

When claimant finally regained consciousness, he was face down in the gutter, and being kicked at to get up by the officers. He was then handcuffed by Officer Rodgers. Disoriented and staggering, claimant was pulled up into a sitting position by the officers. Once seated, the officers then told claimant that "[he was] going to learn [his] place while in Oakland." Officer Rodgers then made several jokes about claimant's inability to breathe when Officer Boyovich was choking him. Claimant then expressed his indignation for being harassed and assaulted. At one point, claimant made a reference to slavery and both officers believing themselves to "master." Officer Rodgers responded with the statement, "I like that (master), I like the sound of that."

Claimant remained handcufffed in a sitting position on the sidewalk in front of the Bank for approximately 20 minutes while waiting for the paddy wagon. When the paddy wagon arrived, claimant was driven around the city of Oakland before reaching the station.

Claimant was jailed for approximately seven (7) hours, cited for resisting arrest, and then released. Claimant suffered from facial abrasions, an aching head, a sore neck, wrists and arms, and muscle soreness from being slammed onto the ground and tightly handcuffed.

The CITY OF OAKLAND and GEORGE HART, Chief of Police for the CITY OF OAKLAND, by and through their supervisory officials and employees, have been given notice on repeated occasions of a pattern of ongoing constitutional violations and practices by Defendants BOYOVICH and RODGERS consisting of the use of unnecessary and excessive force against African American citizens and false arrests of African American citizens. Despite said notice, Defendants CITY OF OAKLAND and GEORGE HART have demonstrated deliberate indifference to this pattern and practice of constitutional violations by failing to take necessary, appropriate or adequate measures to prevent the continued perpetuation of said pattern of conduct by BOYOVICH and RODGERS. Further, Defendants CITY OF OAKLAND and GEORGE HART have failed to adequately train Defendant police officers BOYOVICH, RODGERS and other police officers, in the proper use of force in the course of their employment as police officers. This lack of an adequate supervisorial response and training by Defendants CITY OF OAKLAND and GEORGE HART demonstrates the existence of an informal custom or policy which tolerates and promotes the continuing use of excessive force against and violation of civil rights of African American citizens by BOYOVICH and RODGERS.

Description of nature and extent of injuries and damages: Claimant's physical injuries include but are not limited to:

Pain and injury to his body from being slammed to the ground, face pounded into the pavement, pain and injury to his wrists and arms from the handcuffs, pain and injury to his neck from being choked unconscious, inflicted on him by Defendant BOYOVICH and RODGERS. Claimant was physically and emotionally injured and damaged as a proximate result of this incident.

Claimant's damages include: General, special, punitive, attorney's fees for civil rights violations, and treble damages and $10,000.00 for each offense, pursuant to California Civil Code Section 52(b).

Causes of Action of claimant's complaint may include: Assault, battery, false arrest and imprisonment, violation of California Civil Code Section 51.7, violation of Federal Civil Rights 42 U.S.C. Sections 1981 and 1983, intentional infliction of emotional distress, negligent infliction of emotional distress, and negligence.

DATED: November 12, 1991 LAW OFFICES OF JOHN L. BURRIS

John L. Burris, Esq.
Attorney for Claimant

I HAD NO RECORD ALL MY LIFE. OK? NO RECORD! NO POLICE RECORD UNTIL I MADE A RECORD. AS MY VIDEO WAS DEBUTING ON MTV, I WAS BEHIND BARS GETTING BEAT UP BY THE POLICE DEPARTMENT. I WAS STILL AN N-I-DOUBLE-G-A AND THEY PROVED IT.

All this is scars I go to my grave with. All this is learn-to-be-a-nigga scars.

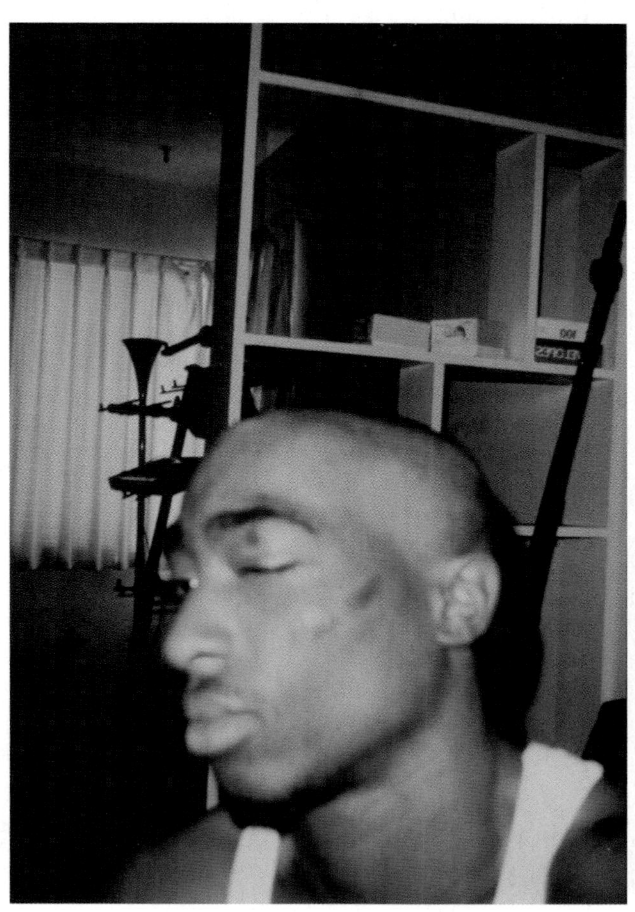

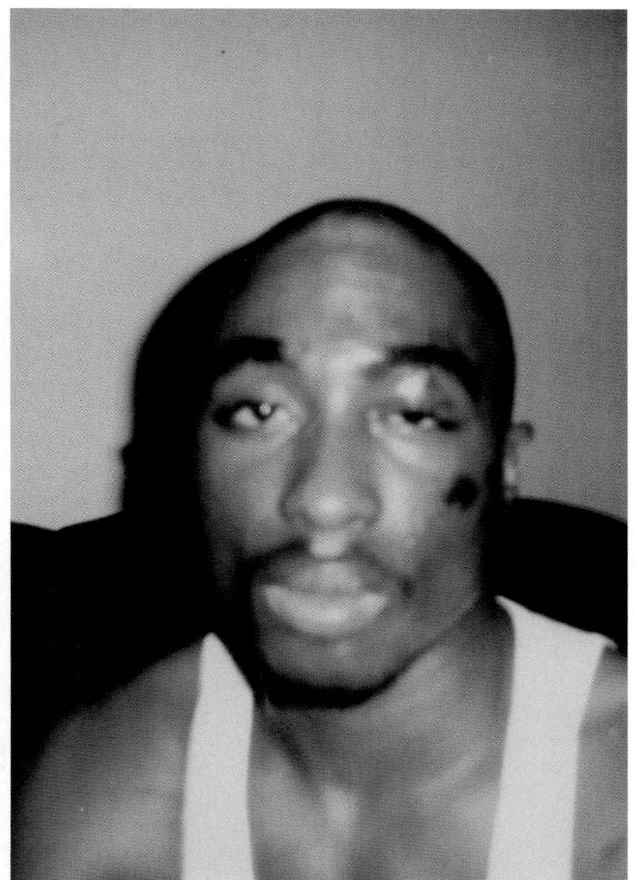

HOLLYWOOD 1992–1994

I AM CRAZY. BUT YOU KNOW WHAT ELSE? I DON'T GIVE A FUCK.

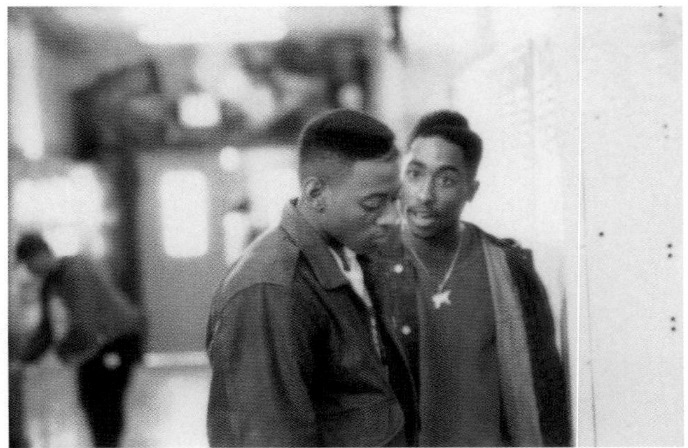

WHEN I AUDITIONED FOR *JUICE*, THAT WAS ANOTHER OF MY GOOD LUCK TIMES. I WAS BROKE. I WASN'T EVEN THINKING ABOUT ACTING. I WAS THINKING ABOUT SURVIVING.

Money B was going to audition. I was just being a sidekick and walked in there wet. Soon as we got home they was like, "We want him to fly back out here," and I was like, if they're going to fly me, I'll go back out there, that's a chance. And then they started, you know, "One more time," and I was like, "OK." All this was good because I hadn't got any parts. I hadn't even gone out on any auditions, so it was like my first audition was going so well.

Bishop is a psychopath, but, more true to his character, Bishop is a lonely, misguided young kid. His heroes are James Cagney and Scarface, those kinds of guys. Shoot-'em-up, go-out-in-a-blaze type of gangsters.

I don't think acting is as technical as they try and make it. They try and make it technical so everybody isn't an actor. All you really have to do is feel for your character and relate to your character. Because when you act you satisfy something inside of yourself.

The character is me, I'm Bishop. Everybody got a little Bishop in them.

I AM REAL. THE LYRICS MIGHT BE A STORY OR THEY MIGHT BE REAL. BUT I STAY REAL, I AM NEVER A STORY, NEVER A SCRIPT, NEVER A CHARACTER. EVEN WHEN I AM PLAYING A CHARACTER I'M REALLY A CHARACTER AT THE SAME TIME. THERE IS NOTHING FAKE.

If Bishop was a reflection of young black males today, I wouldn't be honest if I didn't show another reflection. All of our young black males are not violent, they're all not taking the law into their own hands. Lucky is doing it the opposite way that Bishop did. He's working, he's very responsible. He's very deliberate about the things he's doing. He's taking care of his daughter. He's a respectful person, you know what I'm saying? He lives at home with his mother, he's not sweating it, that's where he wants to be. He wants to work. He wants to set goals and accomplish them.

Lucky the Postman, that was me. I'm the type of person that could be a good father, a good homie, a good son, and a good man at the same time.

I had to tone myself down a lot to be Lucky. But I said, that's what it would take, cuz he's a father and committed to being there for his daughter so he would consciously tone himself down. So I did that. Luckily, I'm a Gemini, so I got both sides.

I DIDN'T HAVE FUN DOING *POETIC JUSTICE*. I DID IT CUZ JOHN WAS MY FRIEND AND I GAVE IT MY ALL BECAUSE HE WAS MY FRIEND. IT WAS HARD. NOT BECAUSE OF JANET, NOT BECAUSE OF NOTHING. IT WAS JUST REALLY HARD AT THAT POINT IN MY LIFE FOR ME TO BE TRYING TO DO A MOVIE. I DON'T THINK I WAS PROFESSIONAL. I THINK I WAS TALENTED BUT I DON'T THINK I WAS PROFESSIONAL. I DIDN'T HAVE THE CONCENTRATION I SHOULD HAVE HAD.

SOX

I LOVE WOMEN. I'M NOT GOING TO LIE. I LOVE WOMEN WITH A PASSION. SOMETIMES I JUST WANNA CALL UP PRINCE AND BE LIKE, "CAN WE HANG?" CUZ I LOVE WOMEN LIKE HE LOVES WOMEN.

I get a lot of friends because I have respect for women. Ultra respect for women. I like being around females, I'm comfortable. I can get with them on every level. I don't get like a predator thing going when I'm around demure females, and I'm not uncomfortable around strong women.

MADONNA IS REAL NICE, SHE'S A GOOD PERSON. SHE HELPED ME A LOT. SHE WAS REAL COOL, LIKE ANY ONE OF MY HOMEBOYS. JASMINE GUY, SHE HELPED. SHE'S A GOOD SUPPORTER.

A sista just to' up, kickin it!
This was a funny day, Remember?

Jaz & Pac Sept 3 '95

JADA'S MY HEART. SHE WILL BE MY FRIEND MY WHOLE LIFE. WE'LL BE OLD TOGETHER. JADA CAN ASK ME TO DO ANYTHING AND SHE CAN HAVE IT. SHE CAN HAVE MY HEART, MY LIVER, MY LUNGS, MY KIDNEYS, MY BLOOD MARROW, ALL OF THAT.

When my mother got clean we got real close again. I don't blame her for anything. My moms is the bomb, you know? World's best mom.

MAMA, I REALLY DO LOVE YOU AND APPRECIATE EVERYTHING YOU'VE DONE FOR ME.

I think my mother taught me to understand women a lot more than my peers can. If you're raised by a woman, you're going to have feminine characteristics. You gonna think like a woman.

But I'm not a woman. I'm just a normal man. I'm very soft, I'm very sensitive. But that's why I'm so harsh, because I'm so sensitive, you know?

TO ME, I'M THE HARDEST MAN AROUND, THE HARDEST NIGGA OUT THERE. BECAUSE I AM REAL. AND I WILL CRY. IF SOMETHING'S BOTHERING ME, I'LL SWING. AND IF I CAN'T BEAT THEM I'LL RUN. I'M NOT STUPID. I'M JUST REAL.

11 18'95

BIRDY JUST HAPPENS TO BE THAT FLAME BUGALOO THE MOTH IS DRAWN TOO. BUGALOO IS HALF A MAN. EVERY HALF A MAN NEEDS A STRONG MAN TO LEAD HIM. HE JUST PROBABLY HAD NO FATHER OR SOMETHING, NO DIRECTION. SO BIRDY BEING THIS STRONG MALE FIGURE, MY CHARACTER JUST LIKE DRAWS ALL THESE MOTHS FROM THE COMMUNITY TO ME AND I LEAD THEM. SORT OF LIKE A GANGBANGING SITUATION.

Except it's just me. Not me Tupac, me Birdy.

BEING FAMOUS AND HAVING MONEY GAVE ME CONFIDENCE. THE SCREAMS OF THE CROWD GAVE ME CONFIDENCE. BEFORE THAT I WAS A SHELL OF A MAN. NOW I BELIEVE THAT I'M MY OWN MAN.

I put it down, I put it down. If it's about rap music, if it's about acting whatever—I want to get into the head set, I gotta be involved, I gotta excel at it. It can't be a small thing, it gotta be a big thing. And I believe that I'm a natural born leader.

I didn't want to change. I love that when I was with Janet Jackson, big movies and all that, I'd be up at the dirtiest house party in the hood.

PEOPLE COULD NOT BELIEVE IT! AND I USED TO THRIVE OFF THAT. BEING UP AT THE PARTY AND SOMEONE TURNING AROUND AND GO, "OH MY GOD, THAT'S TUPAC," AND EVERYBODY GOING CRAZY CUZ I'M UP IN THE DIRTY PARTY, NO SECURITY, LIGHTS OUT, DRINKING. HELLA DRUNK, YOU KNOW, DRUNK WITH EVERYBODY ELSE.

But that's what kept my sanity. That's what kept me writing, that's what kept me going.

32 BOTTLES 2 GHETTO HEAVEN

a screenplay written By T-Shakur

The Jungle was a housing Project. It's name told it all crime arson were usual gunfire chaos and mayhem. 12 Blocks down Santa BayRose was a middle class house. Shadow lived with his grandmother here in BayRose. Teech lived here also. Reese Bluto and Jesse all living in the Jungle. Reese has a biggA brothA whose famous in these parts he's confident. Teech has a family he's intelligent Bluto has a big brothA even more famous than reese and he's a good fighter. Shadow has his Rich Grandmother. Jessie was the oldest child 14 his infant brothA was the really only family member sober enough to notice him his mother & father are both heavy alcoholics who fight constantly. As we open the story we are in Jesse's small room he shares his Room with the baby.

Jesse: Come on Kharee go to sleep. what's wrong? huh u shited on yourself (the baby laughs) oh u like that shit Goddamn MotherfuckA Shit (the baby is giggling as Jesse makes a face 2 each profane word) Damn Fuck Alright enuff (the baby crys again just as Jesse gets in bed) ~~come on~~ Damn Man u a pervert Kharee u hear me a dirty little baby boy with baby nuts and u already got curson problem shit damn MotherfuckA shit damn shit (the baby laughs giggles and finally starts to settle) OKAY GO to bed

In the other Room Jessie's Mother is hitting Jesse's father he's 2 drunk to fight back. She's Really fucking him up. tough woman. Jesse Runs to help his father

THUG LIFE

I WAS SCARED BUT SO WAS AMERICA.

PHILLIES
TITAN
THUG
LIFE
KATO
R.I.P

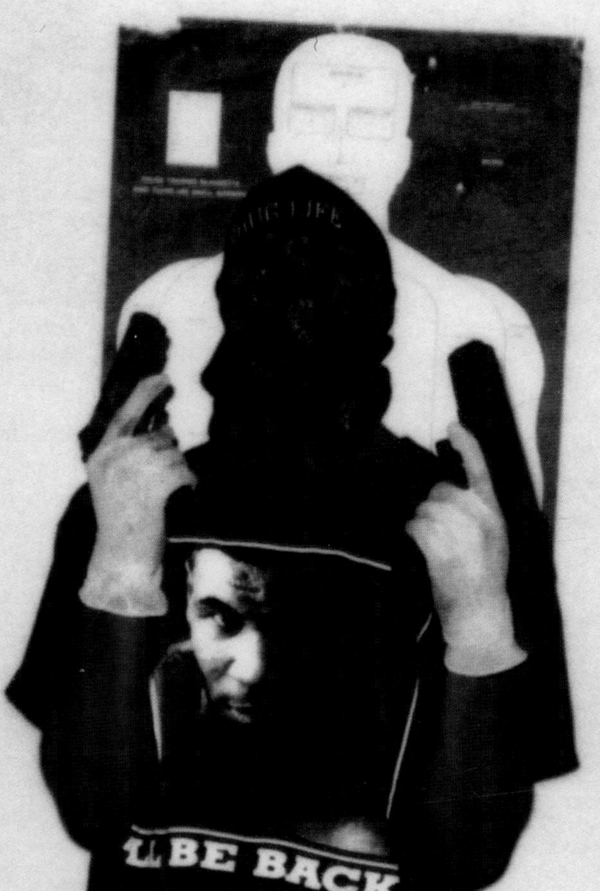
BE BACK

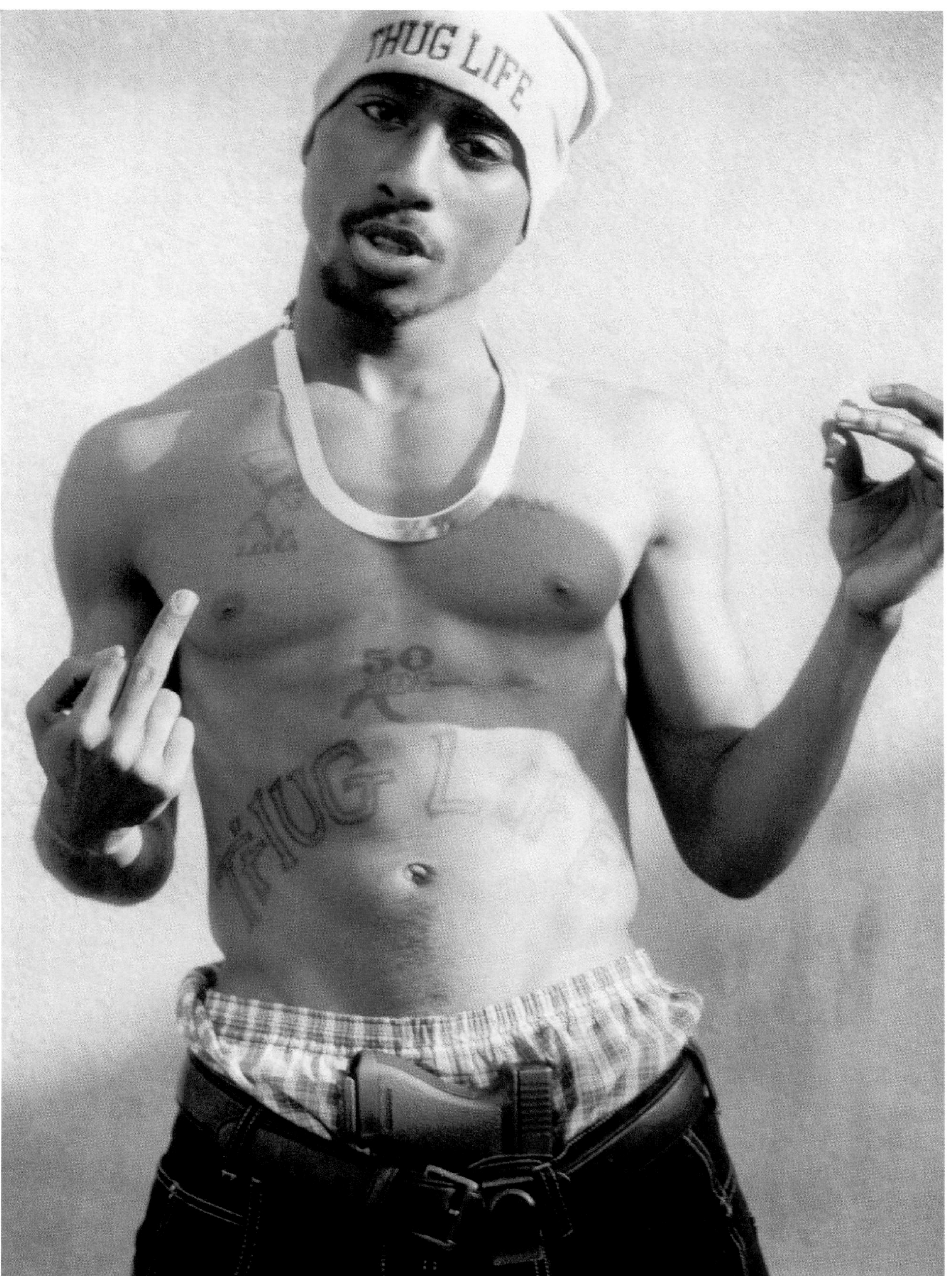
THUG LIFE
THUG

CODE'S OF THE THUG LIFE

Someone must dare put the street life back on track, it's clear to anybody that can see - that the hustling game has gone stark raving mad.

The short and long range result, will not only be detrimental to the street game, but will also destroy any foundation in our community. But more important, the combination of the self destruction and turf warfare, coupled with the government's police terrorism, fascist laws designed to capture and keep our Black men and women in jail for the rest of their lives, and leaves a defenseless community - will result in our genocide.

For as long as the street game / hustle has existed in our community, which is the result of many factors (and will only be resolved through our liberation), it has been viewed as a necessary tolerance between the legal and illegal economy and culture.

The underground economy has in many areas been supportive of the uplifting of the Black community. Although for a fact it has been the down fall of individuals, the dynamic's of struggle between the do-gooders and the thugs has kept a consistent battle for balance in our community which at least was under our control.

The rules of engagement of the hustle - was a code of the thug life. this code was the A, B, C's of how the street game should and would be played. these rules allowed for money to be made by the crews in the different fields of the game, and determined how disputes between and among the players should be handled.

It also allowed the people who were not in the game to pressure the enemy of our people, and allowed the people who would work in the interest of our people (education, health, housing, legal, etc.) to feel that the effort was worth it.

The game today, as it exist, is a complete violation of the code. Historically, the street hustler was hip to the enemy and would never work in the government's interest to destroy their own people.

The thug life is a tool of the enemy as it exist today, it must change. Outside forces and methods whose interests are being served by the hustlers, **the crew have no dignity, they have no honor - and this must be corrected. A counsel must be called to put a code to the thug life.**

We accept that the game will go on until our liberation. What we won't accept is that the game will destroy us from within before we get another chance to rumble and rebuild. We will not allow ourselves to be **played** by the covert operations, contelpro, and low intensity warfare waged by the United States government.

A code must be established, as we look at the **West** coast, the majority of the life is controlled by gangs (Latin / Chicano); the Black community as well, the gangs is the force behind the underground economy in our hoods.

In the mid-**East** the common denominator there is also the gangs, which are responsible for the street life. Politically, culturally, and economically, these forces in an attempt to put the game back on track and work in the **interests** of the community and to resist the strategy of the government. They have begun setting down a platform **for the street game** in full effect - we praise this effort.

The code of the thug life **must** become a part of as well **East** coast street life. There must be a common denominator.

The **original gangsters** behind the walls of the dungeon will take some responsibility to putting force to the counsel and the code...

We must act now. the Code of the Thug Life will save us to fight another day. If we don't - **we're ass out!**

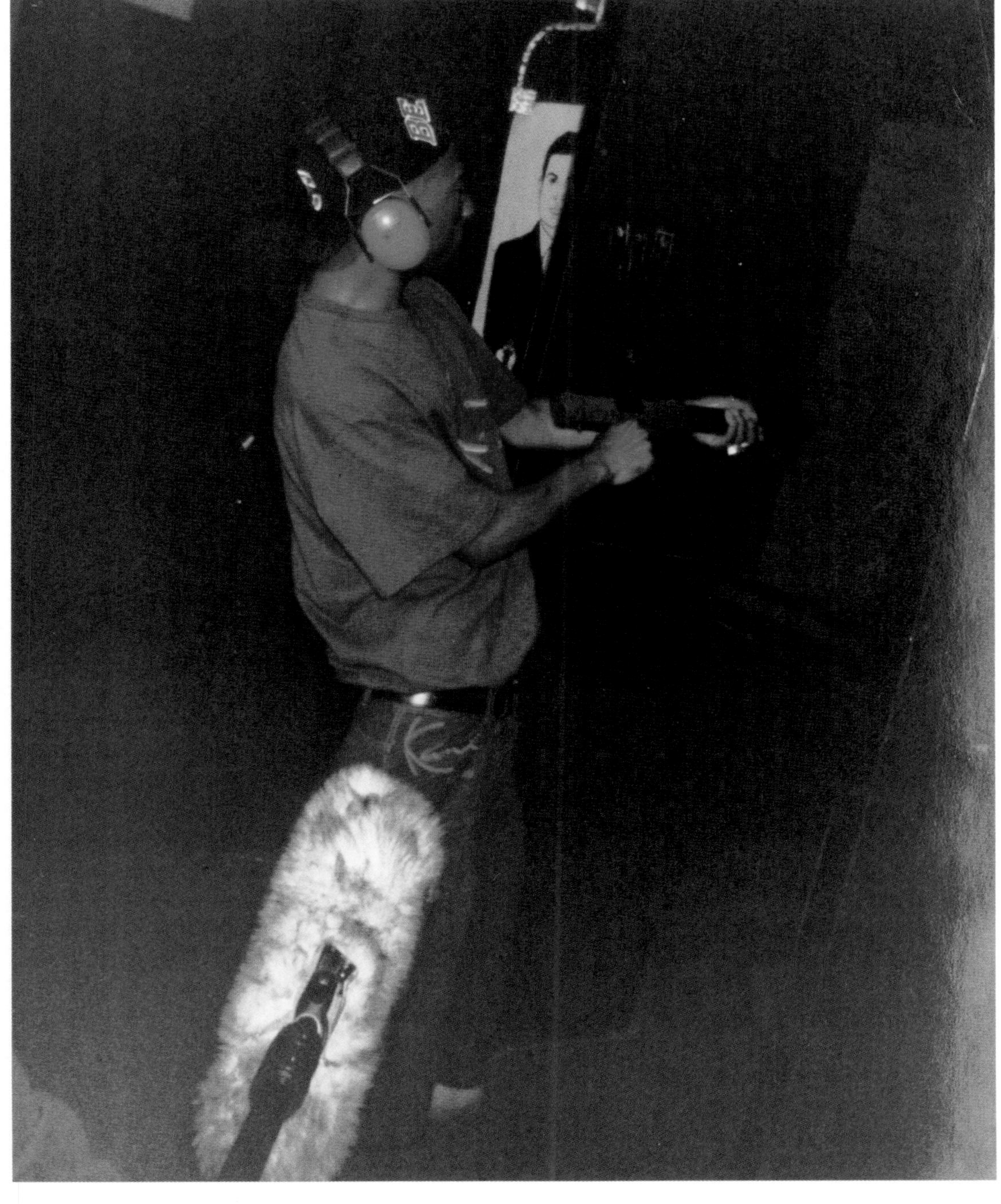

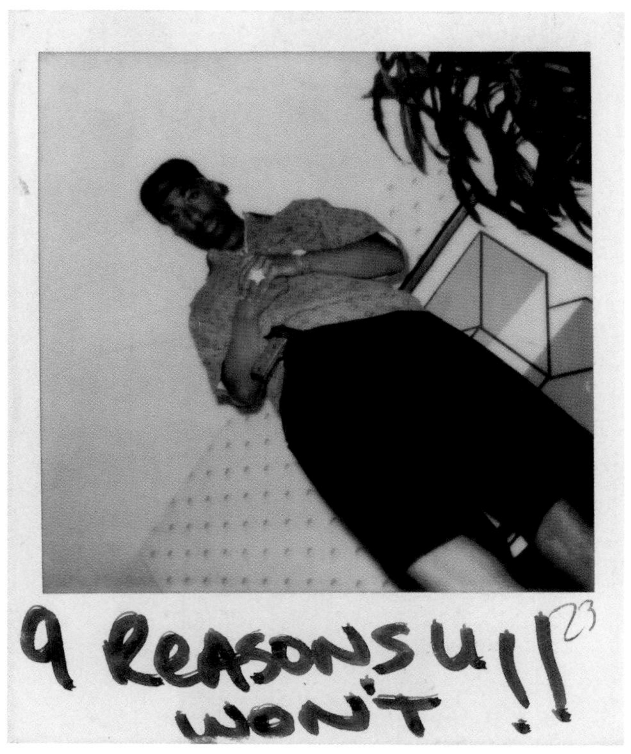
9 REASONS U !!
WON'T

There was no spot for Tupac. It's not like there was somebody like me before and I moved into the spot so I can ask him how he did it. There was no spot here. Nobody wanted to be the person the thugs and the street people could rally around. Nobody wanted to be that. So when I was that, I couldn't handle it. I *could* handle it, but not right away.

I'M TWENTY-TWO. I WAS HAVIN' CONCERTS, THEY WAS SOLD OUT—WHITE BOYS, MEXICANS, BLACKS AND THEY WOULD DO WHATEVER I SAID. I COULD TELL ALL THOSE PEOPLE IN THE AUDIENCE "TURN AROUND IN A CIRCLE" AND THEY WOULD DO IT. I WAS HAVIN' LOVE, UNDENIABLE LOVE, AND I WAS SCARED. I WAS SCARED THAT I WOULD COME TO A TOWN AND I WOULD HAVE THE LEADER OF THE GANG THERE TELLIN' ME, "WHAT DO YOU NEED?"

Of course, I had problems. I was making mistakes that anybody would make when you have fourteen thousand people ready to do whatever you want, when you have people all over the country waiting to hear what you wanna do. I got people in the penitentiary, big time OG criminals, who are callin me, tellin' me they want me to lead their movement. I mean, I'm gonna have a problem. I'm gonna have a small identity crisis here. I was from a single mother. With no father, no male figure. Now I got every man in America who wants to take an order from me, you know what I'm sayin, who wants to know what I want to do, or what's my plan for young black males. And that makes me scared.

BUT THAT MAKES ME WANT TO RISE TO THE OCCASION. MAKES ME WANNA GIVE MY WHOLE LIFE TO 'EM, AND I WILL GIVE MY WHOLE LIFE TO THIS PLAN I HAVE FOR THUG LIFE.

When I say thug I mean not a criminal, someone who beats you over the head, I mean the underdog. You could have two people—one person has everything he needs to succeed and one person has nothing. If the person who has nothing succeeds, he's a thug. Cuz he overcame all the obstacles. Don't ask me why, but it doesn't have anything to do with the dictionary's version of thug. Sorry.

WHEN MY HEART BEATS IT SCREAMS THUG LIFE.

To me thug is my pride, you know what I'm sayin'? Not being someone who goes against the law. Not being someone that takes, but being someone that has nothing and even though there is no home for me to go to, my head is up high, my chest is out, I walk tall, I talk loud, I don't stutter. I'm being strong.

I DON'T UNDERSTAND WHY AMERICA DOESN'T UNDERSTAND THUG LIFE. AMERICA IS THUG LIFE. WHAT MAKES ME SAYING "I DON'T GIVE A FUCK" DIFFERENT THAN PATRICK HENRY SAYING "GIVE ME LIBERTY OR GIVE ME DEATH"? WHAT MAKES MY FREEDOM LESS WORTH FIGHTING FOR THAN BOSNIANS OR WHOEVER THEY WANT TO FIGHT FOR THIS YEAR?

Young black males out there identify with thug life because I'm not trying to clean them up. I am, but I'm not saying come to me clean. I'm saying come as you are. Everybody come as you are and they feel my genuine love for the street elements. I love that, you know what I'm sayin'? I take the good and the bad—we have to work through it, but we can't work together if we not unified.

I organize the OGs in the East Coast and the West Coast and the penitentiaries to come up with a code of ethics for criminals. This thug life code—we have a code putting order to the violence on the streets. I'm not scared to walk in the middle of Watts, Compton, Chicago, wherever and sit down with the OGs and say, "This is what we need to do." I believe they will listen cuz they have thus far. And we got all these people all over the country saying, "Yes, we go by this code."

Like, we gonna be against attacks on people that are not involved with the street gang, with the drug trade or illegal business. You know, all that kidnapping and shooting drive-bys out of the car, we against that.

We sponsor the teams . . . get the churches out there to sell food, and get the fathers and uncles to be security. . . and bring the community spirit back.

WE'LL TRY TO GET A COMMUNITY CENTER IN EVERY GHETTO IN THE COUNTRY THAT HAS THE SAME THINGS AS THEY HAVE IN THE BEVERLY HILLS COMMUNITY CENTER. THEY HAVE A POOL TABLE, A VCR, A LIBRARY. THE KIND OF LIBRARY YOU HAVE AT YALE. IF THEY WANT THE GHETTO TO HAVE BRAINS, GIVE US THE BOOKS!

This is the type of thing young black males can do. We can do anything if you just give us a shot and stop trying to beat us down. I have something to offer to business that hasn't been show before. I have a whole energy that represents not just black youth but white youth, Mexican youth . . . youth!

I GOT PEOPLE ALL OVER THE COUNTRY GETTING "THUG LIFE" ON THEIR STOMACH.

"1999"

By Tupac Shakur

On July 4, 1999, the United States of America as we know it was brought to it's knees by a highly organized military organization known as The New World Society. Led by a charismatic Black man who up until the revolt was the military chief of the Armed forces Charles Patience. His army was made up of renegade members of the Armed forces ~~and~~ mercenariez and organized street gangs of the countries inner cities. On January 3, 2001 the country was once again under the control of the president but for 18 months for the first time in American history there was no America as we know it. The man responsible Charles Patience was also the man who stopped it. On Febuary 17, 2001 he was sentenced to die for treason. He was pardoned by the President and forced to exile in Cuba. Before he left, one person got his story. A female reporter name Gloria Willis. What follows is his story as told to her.

You know those little things they have for the mice where they run around in a circle and there's little blocks for it? Well, society is like that. They'll let you go as far as you want, but as soon as you start asking too many questions and you're ready to change, *boom*—the block'll come.

I'VE GOT THE WHOLE WORLD FEARING ME, YOU KNOW WHAT I'M SAYIN, AT TWENTY-THREE, WEIGHING A HUNDRED AND SIXTY POUNDS. AND I AIN'T EVEN STARTED. I AIN'T EVEN ROLLED MY PLAN OUT YET AND THEY'RE SCARED. I GOT THE VICE PRESIDENT KNOWING WHO I AM, THE PRESIDENT, EVERY COP IN EVERY CITY. AND I HAVEN'T EVEN STARTED WORKING OUT A PLAN.

I BEEN GETTING THE BLAME FOR EVERYTHING THUG LIFE EVER DID. ANYBODY CAN SAY SOMETHING ABOUT THUG LIFE AND IT ALWAYS COMES BACK TO ME. I DONE HAD POLICEMEN GET KILLED AND I GET BLAMED FOR IT. ALL TYPE OF VIOLENCE AND I GET BLAMED FOR IT.

THEY DON'T EVEN KNOW WHAT—THEY JUST TALKING. THEY COULD BE TALKING ABOUT BOB MARLEY FOR ALL THEY CARE. THEY DON'T KNOW WHO THEY'RE TALKING ABOUT. THEY DON'T KNOW WHAT CAREERS THEY'RE HURTING, OR LIVES THEY'RE CHANGING. THEY'RE JUST OUT THERE TRYING TO GET PAID.

I know somebody geesed them up to go attack Tupac, and now what it does is, they attacked a few famous rappers and now they themselves are famous.

I HAVE NOT BROUGHT VIOLENCE TO YOU OR THUG LIFE TO AMERICA. WHY AM I BEING PERSECUTED?

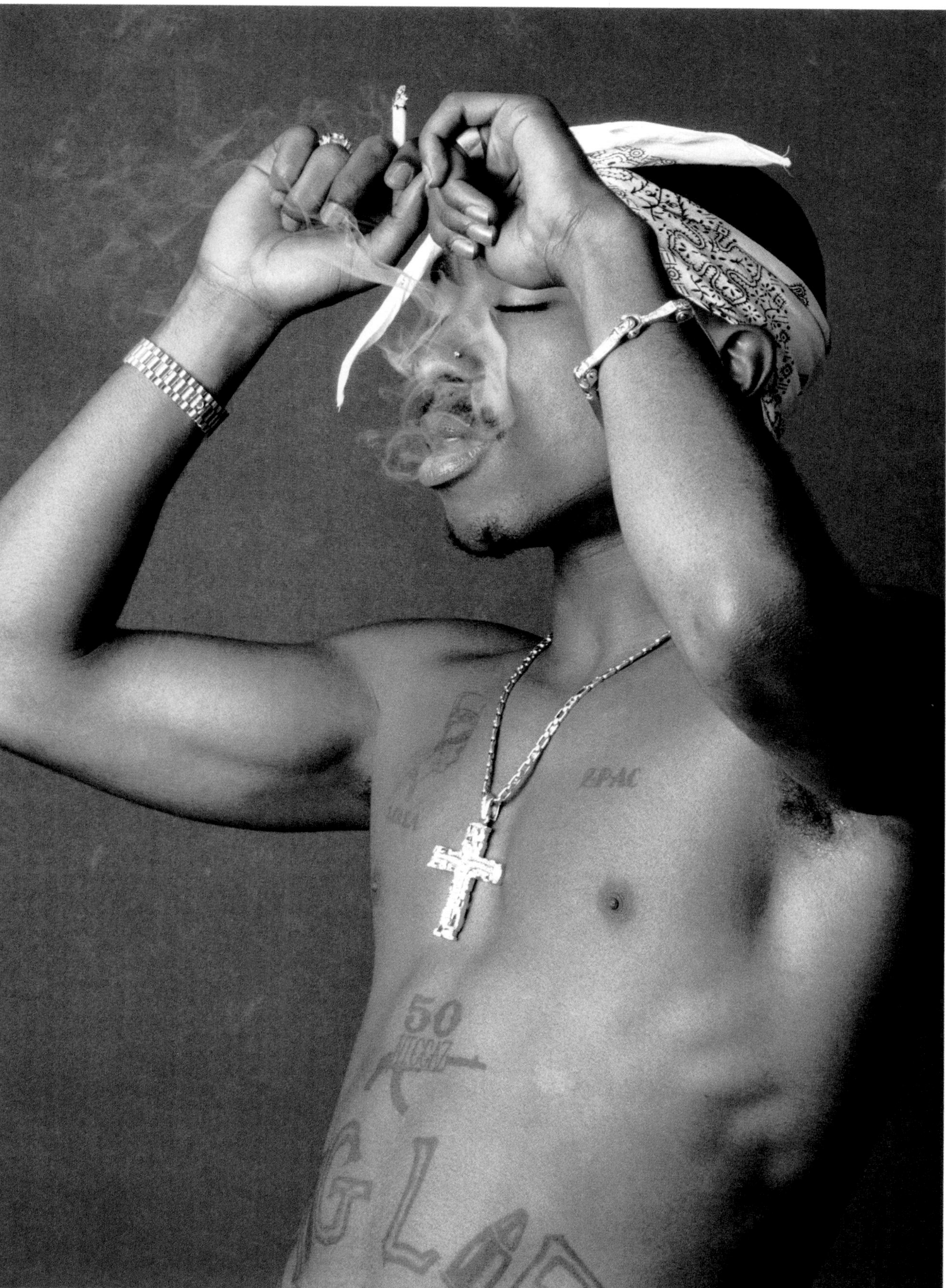
2PAC
50

When did I ever say I was a gangsta rapper?

Is Frank Sinatra a gangsta singer? Is Steven Seagal a gangsta actor? What is that? That's such a limited term. Marlon Brando is not a gangsta actor, he's an actor. Axl Rose and them are not gangsta rock and rollers, they're rock and rollers. So I'm a rapper, this is what I do. I'm an artist. And I rap about the oppressed taking back their place. I rap about fighting back. To me, my lyrics and my verses are about struggling and overcoming, you know? Not gangstas. I don't rap about sitting up eating shrimp and shit. I rap about fighting back.

I MAKE IT UNCOMFORTABLE BY PUTTING DETAILS TO IT. IT MIGHT NOT HAVE BEEN POLITICALLY CORRECT BUT I'VE REACHED SOMEBODY; THEY RELATING TO ME. THEY RELATE TO THE BRUTAL HONESTY IN THE RAP.

And why shouldn't they be angry? And why shouldn't my raps that I'm rappin to my community be filled with rage? They should be filled with the same atrocities that they gave to me.

You have to be logical. If I know that in this hotel room, they have food everyday and I'm knockin' on the door everyday to eat and they open the door and let me see the party—see like them throwin' salami all over, just like throwin' food around—then they're tellin' me there's no food in there, you know what I'm sayin'? Everyday. I'm standing outside trying to sing my way in. "We are hungry, please let us in, we are hungry, please let us in." After about a week that song is going to change to "We hungry, we need some food." After two, three weeks it's like "Give me some food, we're bangin' on the door." After a year it's like, "I'm pickin the lock, comin' through the door blastin'," you know what I'm sayin'? It's like you hungry, you've reached your level. You don't want anymore. We asked ten years ago. We was askin' with the Panthers. We was askin' them with the Civil Rights Movement. We was askin', you know? Now those people who was askin' are all dead or in jail. Now what do you think we're going to do? Ask?

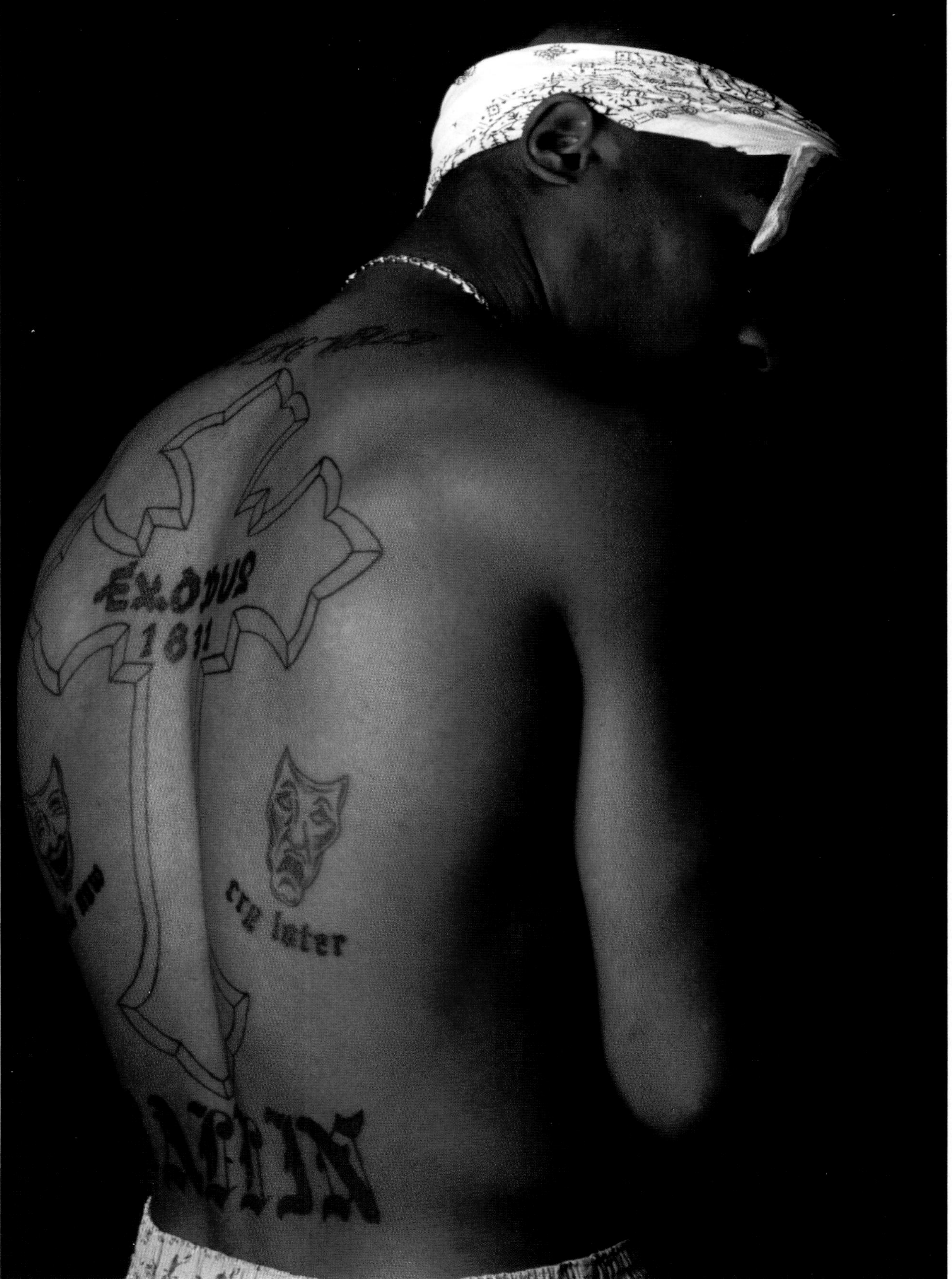
EXODUS
cry later

TRIALS

THAT WAS MY FAULT, THAT I HAD THAT KIND OF ENVIRONMENT AROUND ME.

SOMEBODY ASKED ME, "YOU EXPLOIT WOMEN?" AND, I MEAN, I MIGHT—WITH HER PERMISSION—I MIGHT SMACK A GIRL ON HER BUTT IN THE VIDEO. I MIGHT BE DRINKING CHAMPAGNE OR DRINKING SOMETHING LIKE THAT. BUT EVERYTHING IN MODERATION.

I don't always have to do a song where there's the good woman. I don't see it as women being all one thing . . . I think that all women are different.

And if I do something that has a bad woman, then people go, "Oh, he hates women." No, look, OK? I don't! But I think there is definitely a type of female—label them a bitch—who, their main thing is to get what they can get and they revel in breakin' a nigga's heart, taking what he owns, and, you know, making a man, ruining a man. There's male bitches too.

WOMEN KNOW THERE ARE BITCHES OUT THERE. I DON'T KNOW WHY WOMEN LOOK SURPRISED FOR US TO BE SAYING THAT THERE ARE BITCHES OUT THERE. THEY KNOW—THEY SAY IT LOUDER. THEY JUST THINK THAT WE'RE SAYING THEY'RE ALL BITCHES. THAT'S NOT WHAT WE'RE SAYING.

And that's what I tried to do with "Keep Ya Head Up" and "Get Around." I said, "I'ma write a song about women like my mom, or the women like my sister, who I think represent a strong black woman," and I did that. Now I'm gonna rap about the women I see everyday, and that was "Get Around."

If I just did songs like "Keep Ya Head Up" it would make me seem more than what I am, but I'm just a normal man. I have sex with people, I make love to people I love. But I still enjoy having sex without the emotional connection because the connection I have would be passion, or attraction, or lust, something like that.

orm CRC 133 Rev. 2-1-72

BAIL BOND
520.20 - CPL

CRIMINAL COURT OF THE CITY OF NEW YORK

Part AR3 County NY

93N092783
Docket Number

11-24-93
Adjourned Date

THE PEOPLE OF THE STATE OF NEW YORK

F
Adjourned Part

State of New York)
) ss.:
County of NY)

vs.

TUPAC SHAKUR

An accusatory instrument having been filed in this Court on 11-19, 1993,

charging TUPAC SHAKUR, the defendant herein,

with the offense of PL 130.50(1), 110-130.50(1), 130.65(1)

and bail having been fixed in the amount of FIFTY THOUSAND ($50,000.00) Dollars:

(I) (We), TUPAC SHAKUR, the defendant herein,

residing at 23236 W. LYONS BLVD, NEWHALL CA,

by occupation a ACTOR,

She did some things there at the club and we got together later that night. I saw her again another time with these guys who introduced me to her.

EVERYBODY WAS HAVING A GOOD TIME, NOTHING SEXUAL—JUST EVERYBODY HAVING A GOOD TIME. ME AND HER WENT IN THERE, SHE GAVE ME A MASSAGE, CAME OUT. WENT TO SLEEP, WOKE UP, SHE'S SCREAMING "RAPE! RAPE!" I RAPED HER. SHE'S YELLIN' AT ME, "THIS ISN'T THE LAST YOU'RE GONNA SEE OF ME." I'M CURSING HER OUT CUZ I'M NOT THINKING SHE'S REALLY GONNA DO THAT. AND THE NEXT THING I KNOW I'M GOING TO JAIL.

I'm not capable of doing any harm to a woman—that's really the main thing, you know what I'm sayin'? I do mess around, I do act crazy, I do get drunk, I do have parties, I do get into little fistfights with guys, but I'm not capable of doing any harm to a woman. Taking something from her, that's not me, that would never be me. They don't have to worry about me hurting kids or a woman or anything like that. That's not me; I'm a victim. I would never make anybody a victim. That's not me.

I DON'T HAVE ANY FRIENDS ANYMORE. I'M SURROUNDED, BUT I DON'T HAVE ANY FRIENDS. I HAVE HOMIES, ASSOCIATES.

What relationship could I possibly have? Now I'm petrified; I can't mess with women. Now, I'm vulnerable cuz they all like, "Ah ha! You're in trouble." So I just decided to withdraw myself.

I CAN'T GO TO CLUBS ANYMORE. NOW I'M JUST A PRISONER TO MY OWN FAME. I CAN'T GO OUT, I CAN'T MEET NICE GIRLS. I CAN'T GO ANYWHERE, I CAN'T GO TO BARBECUES ANYMORE, I CAN'T GO TO SCHOOL.

And it's fake, it's messed up. I can't do shows. Everybody's already "I'm guilty" . . . but I can't even go to Philly, I can't go to Texas. I can't go nowhere, I can't go nowhere. That's why I wanted to die at that point. I was like "Fuck, shit, I'm tired." At twenty-two, I'm tired.

I should be rejuvenated, young and twenty-two, and just entering college—just leaving college or something. When I'm just starting my life. I'm just starting to build a future for my family, for their family, you know what I'm saying? When I started seeing that, it made me say, "It's hopeless."

I wasn't like one day waking up and wanting to commit suicide; it was like all around I felt suicidal. But I couldn't kill myself. I just wanted somebody to kill me for me. But I also thought, "I cannot die with people thinking I'm a rapist or criminal. I can't leave until this shit is straight."

But it's also like suicide because you're so tired you want to sleep. I'm like a victim, a target—so I couldn't sleep, I couldn't rest. I couldn't sleep at home; people kill me at home, police gonna come and kill me? Is there secret police? I'm just paranoid. I was so deep into weed at that point. I'm bugging out because I'm such a menace to everybody.

IN GOD
WE TRUST
Freedom
I AM
INNOCENT

Shepard

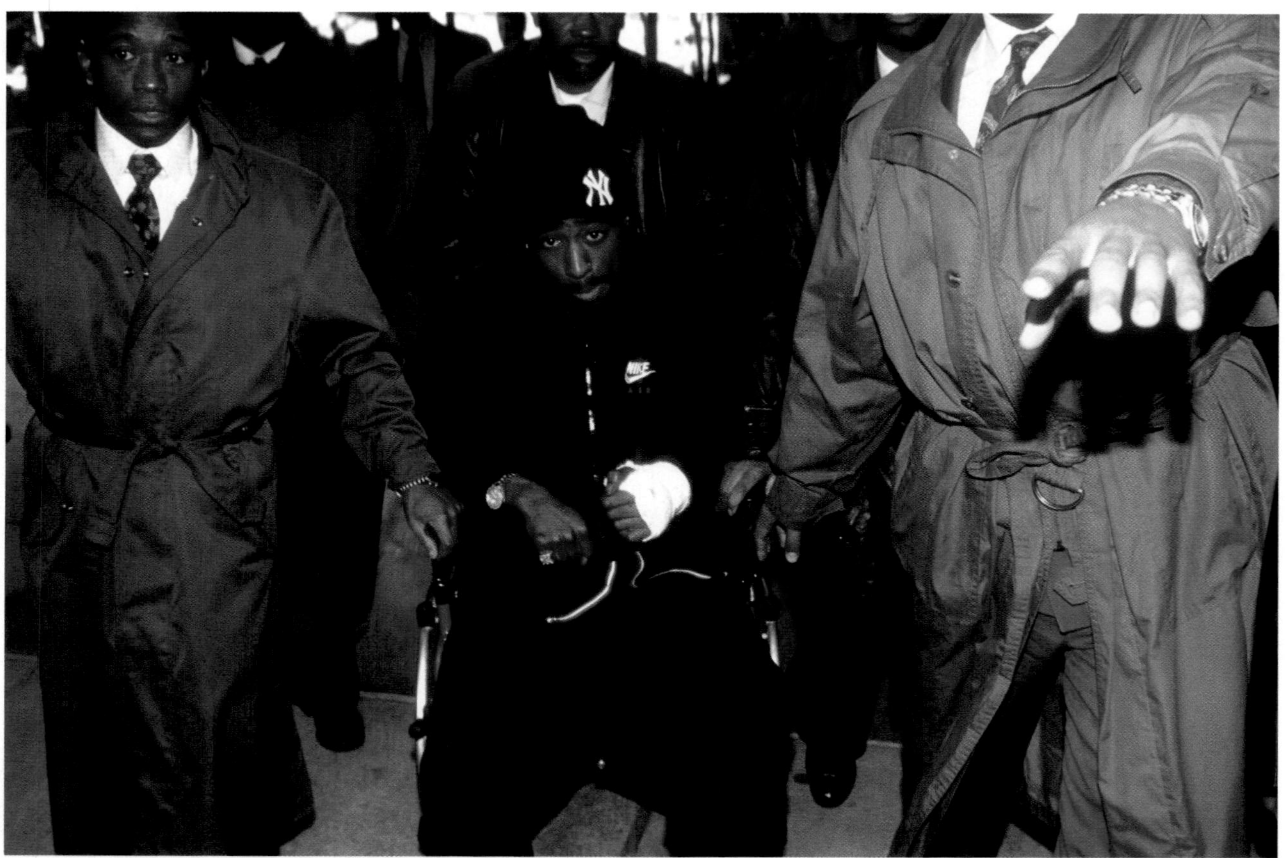
NIKE

I GOT SHOT FIVE TIMES. I WALKED IN, SOME DUDES WALKED IN AND SHOT ME UP, TOOK SOME JEWELRY. I HAVE NO IDEA WHY THEY SHOT ME.

When I wasn't dead immediately, I was like, "Oh man!" I was like, "Naw, this ain't it. I know how it's gonna be when I die. There's gonna be no noise, you're not going to hear people screaming. I'm gonna fade out." None of that was there. I got shot five times, I'm not dead, they missed, I'm back.

I KNOW WHO SHOT ME. EVERYBODY KNOWS WHO SHOT ME. THE POLICE KNOW WHO SHOT ME.

THE SITUATION WITH ME IS LIKE, WHAT COMES AROUND, GOES AROUND. KARMA. I BELIEVE IN KARMA, I BELIEVE IN ALL OF THAT. I'M NOT WORRIED ABOUT IT, YOU KNOW? THEY MISSED. I'M NOT WORRIED ABOUT IT UNLESS THEY COME BACK.

Shepard
12/1/94

Am I crazy or what? Hell no, I ain't crazy. I was pissed off. What's really going on is, this is a crazy world and if you're not a tad bit crazy then you cannot survive. You will not survive, you will not be able to look at the news, you will not be able to meet people, you will be in the house with your doors locked. You've got to be a little crazy and I think I am. I'm crazy enough to deal with this bullshit.

FIRST I WAS LIKE, "I'M NOT GOING TO JAIL." IF THEY TRY TO COME GET ME FOR SOMETHING I DIDN'T DO, I'M GONNA OPEN FIRE, YOU KNOW WHAT I'M SAYIN'? BUT I CAN'T DO THAT BECAUSE IT'S NOT JUST ME ANYMORE, AND THAT'S WHAT THEY EXPECT.

If I have to, if God sees it fit for me to spend time in a cell, if he wants my brain to be inside of a cage, if he's brought me so far from hell to put me here and now he wants me to go to jail, I'll go.

IF THAT'S WHERE I'M MEANT TO BE, BUT I DON'T THINK SO. I DON'T BELIEVE IN MY HEART THAT I BELONG IN JAIL.

PRISON 1995

I LEARNED THINGS THERE.

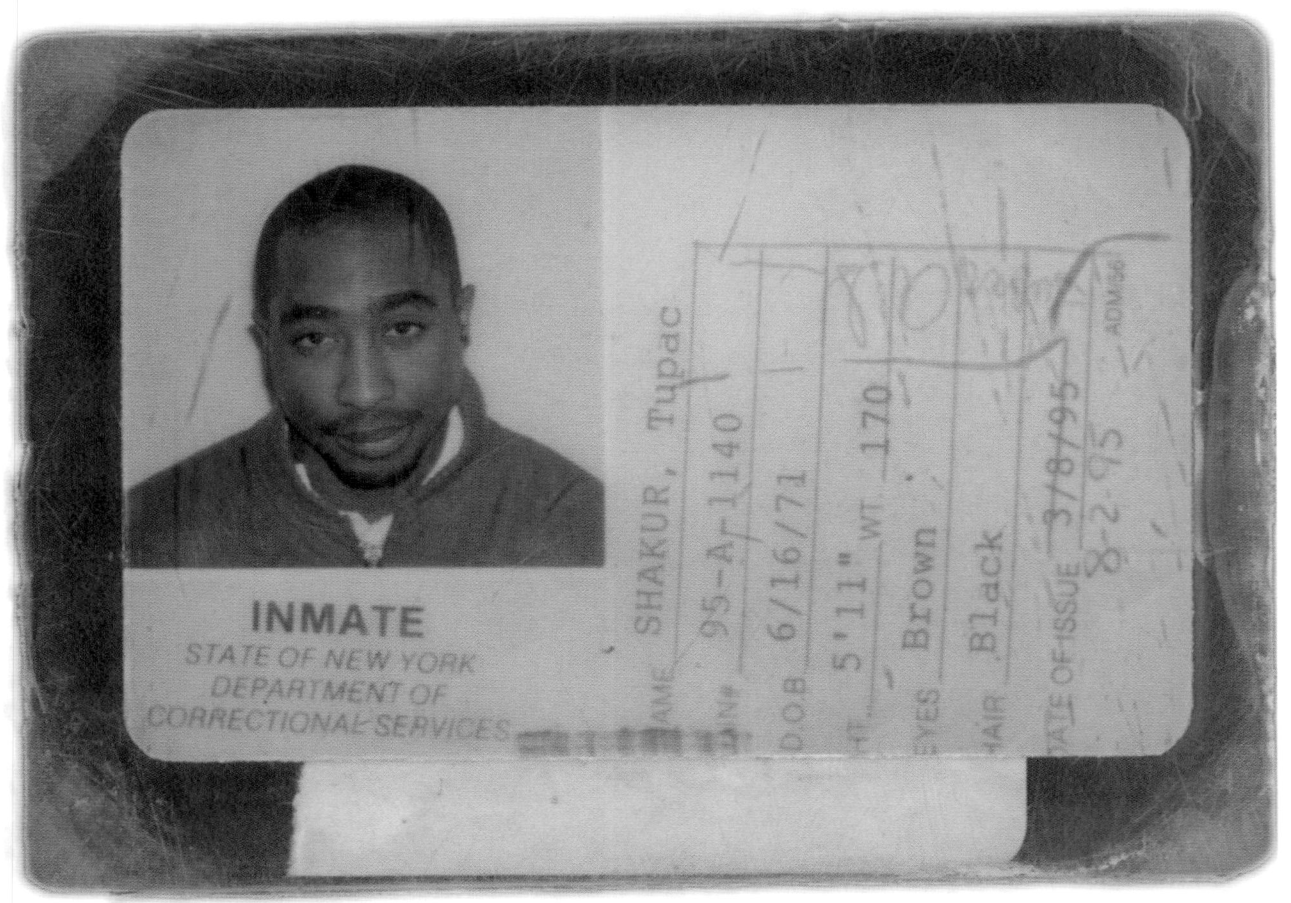
INMATE
STATE OF NEW YORK
DEPARTMENT OF
CORRECTIONAL SERVICES
SHAKUR, Tupac
95-A-1140
D.O.B 6/16/71
5'11" WT 170
EYES Brown
Black
3/8/95
8-2-95

I DON'T HAVE ANY PROBLEMS TELLING PEOPLE IT'S NOT COOL TO GO TO JAIL, CUZ I BEEN THERE, AND IT'S NOT COOL.

WHERE I WAS AT WAS A MAXIMUM SECURITY PENITENTIARY WHERE EVERYBODY, THE TOP OF THE LINE, GOES. THIS IS WHERE THEY SEND YOU. IF YOU WERE TO KILL SOMEBODY IN NEW YORK, OR HAD BLEW UP THE WORLD TRADE, THIS IS WHERE THEY WOULD HAVE SENT YOU.

The way they explained it was, I was too famous to go to a medium or minimum.

That doesn't make sense. If I'm too famous to go to a regular jail, I'm too famous to be in jail. Put me under house arrest, you know what I mean? They don't send Tupac to that.

Major

curl 25 4 setz 5 each arm
curl 35 2 setz of 5 each arm
Bench wing curl 35 5 timez each side
chest 90 10 timez 100 5 times
Dipz 3 setz of 10
crunchez 3 setz of 10
WINGZ 70 5 timez (3 setz)
legz 10 setz of 5

~~Minor~~

chest push 100 5 times 5 sets
curl 25 10x on each arm 5 sets
curl 35 5 timez each arm 5 sets
chest push 90 10 times 5 sets
pull downz 50 poundz 10 timez (5 setz)
40 poundz 20 timez (5 setz)
Dipz 3 setz 10
crunchez 5 setz of 10
Chesh push 100 5 times
wing 5 x 50 3 sets

So now I'm basically more scared of people than guns. I trust NO-ONE!! As far as Riker's it has it's ups and downs. THERE IS ALOT OF JEALOUSY!! Mostly from the C.O.'s. As far as this race war. I have been, for the most part sheltered from it. the LATINOS I do come across show me the utmost respect. they offer razors, shanks, food, whatever! What Do I think of unification? I have a hard time believing Brothas can unite let alone Brothas and LATINOS but if it could happen it would be my dream. They have alot of "gangs" up here but me being aware of how true the gang situation is in L.A. These niggas in here are comical! Dangerous! but comical.

INSTITUTIONAL RULES OF CONDUCT

100 Assault and Fighting

		Tier
100.10	Inmates shall not assault, inflict or attempt to inflict bodily harm upon any other inmate.	II, III
100.11	Inmates shall not assault, inflict or attempt to inflict bodily harm upon staff member.	II, III
100.12	Inmates shall not assault, inflict or attempt to inflict bodily harm upon any person not included in rules 100.10 and 100.11.	II, III
100.13	Inmates shall not engage in fighting.	II, III
100.14	Inmates shall not practice or instruct others in martial arts (aikido, judo, karate, juijitsu, kung fu, tai chi chu'an, etc.)	I, II, III
100.15	Inmates shall not engage in unauthorized sparring, wrestling, body punching, or other forms of disorderly conduct	I, II

105.12	Inmates shall not engage or encourage others to engage in unauthorized organizational activities or meetings, display, wear, possess, distribute or use unauthorized organizational insignia or materials. An unauthorized organization is any gang or an organization which has not been approved by the Deputy Commissioner for Program Services.	I, II, III

106 Refusal to Obey a Direct Order

		Tier
106.10	**ALL ORDERS OF FACILITY PERSONNEL WILL BE OBEYED PROMPTLY AND WITHOUT ARGUMENT.**	I, II, III

107 Interference with an Employee or other Persons

		Tier
107.10	Inmates shall not physically or verbally obstruct or interfere with an employee at any time.	I, II, III
107.11	Inmates shall not harass employees or any other persons verbally or in writing. This includes, but is not limited to, using insolent, abusive and/or obscene language and gestures, or writing or otherwise communicating messages of a personal nature to employees or volunteers.	I, II, III

SO I'M UP IN HERE, IN JAIL, WHERE YOU'RE SUPPOSED TO BE GOOD AT, NO WEAPONS, YOU'RE PAYING FOR YOUR SINS, DUDES IS GETTING KILLED. DUDES IS COMIN' IN THERE WITH ONE AND A HALF TO FOUR AND A HALF, GETTING STABBED IN THE CHEST WITH A PAIR OF SCISSORS, AND DYING IN JAIL, AND NEVER COMING HOME.

I WAS JUST IN JAIL WITH THESE DUDES. I SEEN, I MEAN YOU WOULD NOT BELIEVE IT. TWICE THIS HAPPENED—MURDERS IN JAIL. IT WAS IN ANOTHER SECTION OF THE JAIL. BUT IT'S HAPPENED, THEN THEY LOCK THE JAIL DOWN AND WE CAN'T MOVE AROUND.

For the first half of my stay there, me and the guards had problems. I got smacked, treated bad . . . they just did everything they could do to try and break me because I used to talk a lot of shit.

As soon as I got there they went, "There's the rich nigger." I was like, "Oh, shit! He said 'nigger'! He said 'nigger'!" And everyone was looking at me like, "So?" I was like, "Oh my God, this is where I'm gonna be staying? He just said 'nigger'!"

He talking about niggers. Niggers was the ones on the rope hanging out the thing. Niggaz is the ones with the gold ropes hanging out at the clubs. If you're not a nigga . . . you don't use that word.

MY INSPIRATION WAS GONE BECAUSE I WAS A CAGED ANIMAL.

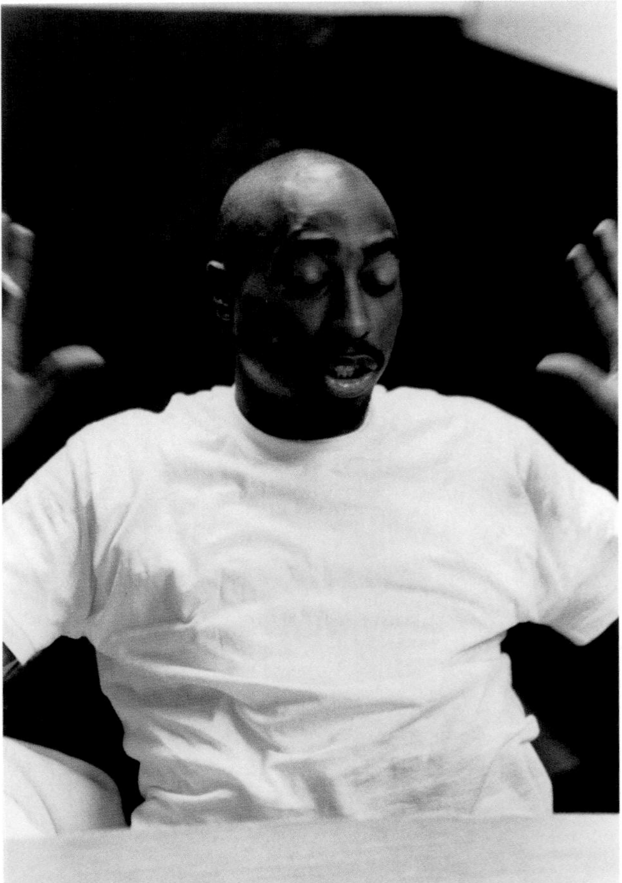

NOTHING Gold

Panaramic

EXT. Nighttime. Breezy Autumn Winds blow fragile Amber leaves through the Suburban street. Carrigan street is legendary for it's perfectly trimmed grass & it's peaceful disposition It was the type of place that made you happy to be away from the stress of the city, Even if it was just 26 miles Away from New York. This was like a whole different world A place where kidz play & parents attend P.T.A. and everybody Knows everybody. **KARLO** KIEDA, and his Mother DELORES had just moved from the Bronx tenemants to live with her new husband and his new step father.

— Voice Over —

When my mother said she was getting married again my stomach knotted up like you couldn't imagine, not that I wasn't happy for my mom but I knew why she was doing it. She lost her job and my Brother Jerry needed to go to a ~~[illegible]~~ Home for mentally retarded ~~kids~~ Adults Then she started going out alot, And whenever my mother got all dressed up and puts on heels and make up I start counting down the days before the wedding and Sure as shit JUNE 16 my mother became MRS Donald Jones At first Don was cool but aren't they all in the beginning. We went fishing, he took me to Knicks games, target shooting (DON ~~is~~ a cop) everywhere. He was the perfect step father, At least I was led to believe he was, And it's funny because as soon as I told my mother how cool he was and after they were married everything changed.

handheld

Insert → Wedding Scene Everyone laughing and happy except two Boys Sitting alone at A table obviously mopping This is Jerry & Karlo

INT. Nighttime The Jones' house. C/U on the face of GIANCARLO WATTS ~~A yes~~ 16 AS He lays awake staring at the cieling. ~~[illegible]~~ the Rapturous ~~[illegible]~~ sounds of his mother & Don having sex vibrates through the walls causing a rythmic lullaby as it knocks against his headboard. Unable to sleep he does what he often does.. day dream!

"KINDRED SPIRITS"

By Tupac Shakur (loosely based on a Novel by OCTAVIA E. Butler)

ESTABlishing Shot - Manhattan New York - MORNING - Sometime in our future.

The Jagged Skyline surrenders to the glorious signs of dawn. Curious pigeons scatter and fly over the skyscrappers as we come to a highrise apartment. Through the slightly open window we see a beautiful black woman of her 20's standing naked and proud as she smokes vigorously from a cigarette. Her SKIN glows from the morning light and her Vulumptuous body bears no flaws. Her breast full and high heaves with her every breath. Her legs look like those of an olympic runner · chiseled & well developed. Her eyes, emerald green and as intoxicating as the strongest liqour. Her long wavy hair hung effortlessly over her soft shoulders she was the epitome of Beauty. A woman like no other. Her name was DALANI SUKARI.

INT - APT. Bedroom - DAY

The Bedroom is immaculate. A half burned candle sits immersed in wax on a bedstand and several condomn packages lay torn open & strewn about. A silk evening gown lays thrown on a chair along with several articles of men's cloths. A picture of a middle Aged white man and his blonde wife sits perched beside the candle. As Dalani grabs the evening gown and walks into the bathroom we pass by the body of the man in the picture with a perfect bullethole above his left eye

THE FIRST EIGHT MONTHS, I SPENT IN SOLITUDE, TWENTY-THREE-HOURS-A-DAY LOCKDOWN, READING, WRITING. I WROTE A SCRIPT CALLED *LIVE TO TELL*.

I read *Screenplay,* that big famous book by Syd Field. I got that and I remembered all the scripts I'd ever read, and I wrote one. It's based semi on my own life and the rest is fiction. But it follows this guy through his whole life. It's a coming-of-age story. But it tells the mother's side of view. It's like a movie to all of my albums.

—

FRANK & Jesse

ESTABlishing Shot: Marin County, California
The Beautiful landscape of the quiet county is intoxicating to behold. In the center of the town was the county Jail.

Ext - County Jail - Day
a few haggard women walk aimlessly into the Jail to visit forgotten loved ones. Sitting on a park Bench wearing A Walkman over his long blond hair, nodding furiously to Megadeath, JESSE JAMES, watches the door. He's wearing an indian Suede vest and tattered Jeans with cowboy boots. A heavyset black woman in her 20's looks at Jesse and he we motions for her to go inside. The Woman enters the Jail.

Int - County Jail - Day

MY BROTHER'S KEEPER

BY T. SHAKUR

ESTABLISHING SHOT: BOSTON U. EARLY MORNING

~~EXT~~. The Autumn leaves blow aimlessly over the busy college campus ~~as~~ the students of Boston University run to make it for thier first class

INT ART CLASS - DAY

Twenty or so students sit in a circle while a naked woman holds her pose. Several immature students snicker as the class goes on ~~but~~ one student look attentively at the woman recording her every inch. his EASEL holds the canvas of his work. The form of the woman is already masterfully sketched as NICHOLAS ST. JOHN begins to bring life to the lifeless figure. The Professor walks around the room and looks at several pictures in progress ~~He~~ Stops at LAURA PAGNOTTI's ~~pa~~ canvas and shakes his head in disgust.

— PROFESSOR —

NO, NO this is all wrong ms pagnotti
I don't think your trying.

— LAURA — (laughing)

I am trying but Professor
I need something to inspire
me ... Maybe we could have one
of the guys ~~up~~ there. then Leonardo DIVINCI lookout

The class laughs. The Professor walks over to Nick's canvas and holds it up

— PROFESSOR —

MS Daniels you can take a break (The model steps down)

JAIL IS BIG BUSINESS. BELIEVE ME, I SEE THE BIG BUSINESS. THEY CHARGE YOU FOR YOUR TELEPHONE CALLS. THEY CHARGE YOU FOR DISCIPLINARY PROBLEMS. JAIL IS BIG BUSINESS. YOU KNOW, YOU COULD FEED A WHOLE TOWN OFF ONE JAIL.

This jail is in the middle of a town that feeds everybody. Everybody works here. This is the main income. You can buy safety. You can put money in your account. And I make sure just for the guards' sake that I keep about $5,000 in my account or something. So when you got that money in your account, you can buy something when you go to the commissary. I became the most generous person in there. When I left, I left everything I owned to other people. From the TV, to the Walkman, everything. You can have all this. I was like that while I was in there. Getting food, whatever I had, I'd share or whatever.

I had this guy used to cook for me—this guy named Sodo. He used to make rigatoni, and spaghetti and meatballs, everything. I had Italian guys making food, so I ate good. It's illegal, but that's what they do. And dudes be eating rice and everything. Everything.

I learned things there. Like when Al Sharpton came to visit me, he had marched against most of the guys I was friends with in jail. Not friends, like in that word, "friend," but who I associated with. And I would have to explain to him in jail it's like a whole different thing, like how you should be in life—humble. Because this guy was like—I was talking to skinheads and everything. Cuz you don't like black people, alright, that's fine. That's your opinion. Just like I want people to respect my opinion when I'm rapping, I'm gonna respect your opinion. But I want you to treat me with respect, and I'll treat you with respect. And we get along good. This guy, the skinhead, hate black people all over, he getting autographs for his little cousins. I felt like I accomplished something. I know by him getting my autograph, that meant something to me. He couldn't hate black people and come get my autograph, you know what I mean?

For that brief moment my record got released, I was the number one record. People made me number one. And I loved them for that.

IT WAS A TRIP, IT WAS A TRIP. EVERY TIME THEY USED TO SAY SOMETHING BAD TO ME, I'D BE LIKE, "THAT'S ALRIGHT, I GOT THE NUMBER ONE RECORD IN THE COUNTRY." CUZ THEY USED TO TELL ME STUFF LIKE, "YOU'RE IN JAIL, WON'T BE ANY MORE RAPPING FOR A LONG TIME FOR YOU, HUH? HA, HA, HA." I'D BE LIKE, "WELL, ACTUALLY, MY ALBUM IS NUMBER ONE IN THE COUNTRY RIGHT NOW. I JUST BEAT BRUCE SPRINGSTEEN."

And they used to be like, "Go back to your cell." Plus, I used to get *Entertainment Weekly* **in the mail and just read and see where my record was and just trip out. Be like, "Damn! Number one. In the whole country." To me, it'll always be my favorite album.**

Me Against the World **was really to show people that this is an art to me. That I do take it like that. And whatever mistakes I make, I make out of ignorance, not out of disrespect to music or the art. So** *Me Against the World* **was deep, reflective.**

It was like a blues record. It was down-home. It was all my fears, all the things I just couldn't sleep about. Everybody thought I was living so well and doing so good that I wanted to explain it. And it took a whole album to get it all out. I get to tell my innermost, darkest secrets. I tell my own personal problems.

It's explaining my lifestyle, who I am, my upbringing and everything. It talks about the streets but it talks about it in a different light. There's a song on there dedicated to mothers, just a song I wrote just for my mother. And it digs deeper like that. I just wanted to do something for all the mothers. I'm proud of that song. It affected a lot of people.

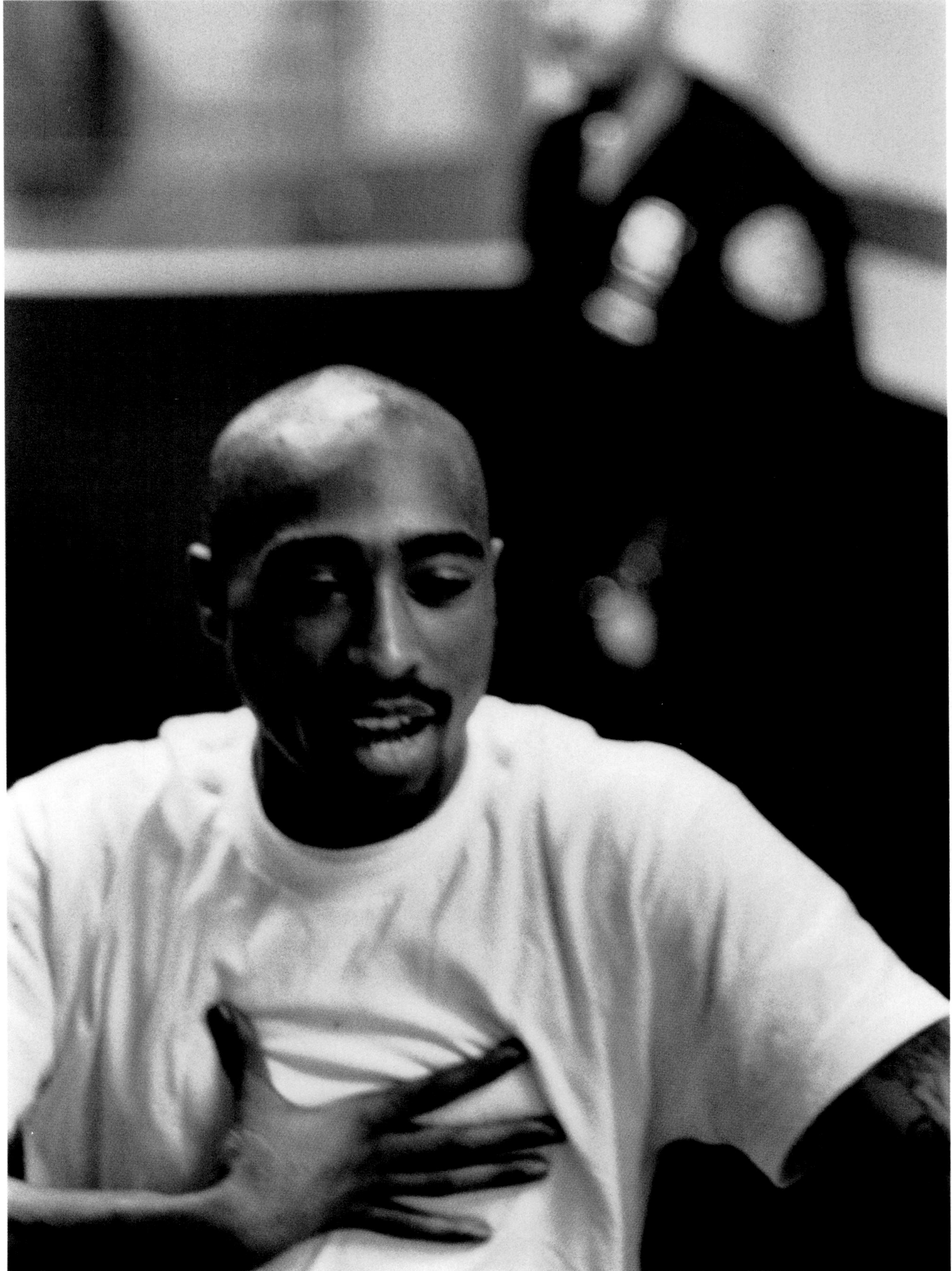

2PAC
"Me Against the World"

Side A

INTRODUCTION

1) If I Die 2nite
* 2) Me Against the World (used in BAD BOYS soundtrack)
* 3) So Many TearZ Single (Show song)
* 4) Temptation club Single
5) Young Nigga (Show Song)
6) Heavy in the Game w/ Richie Rich
7) Lord Knowz

Side B

* 1) Dear Mama 1st Single (Show Song)
2) It Aint eazy
* 3) Can U get Away 2nd Single (Show Song)
4) Old School B-Side
5) Phuck The World (Show Song)
6) Death Around the Corna'
7) OUTLAW featuring DRAMACYDAL (Show Song)

~~Ke~~ 1 Phuck The World
2 So Many Tears
3 Young Nigga
4 Can u get Away
5 Dear mama
6 ~~Keep Ya Head~~ Outlaw
7 Keep Ya ~~Head~~ Up

Dear Mama

— treatment —

Along With Whatever ideas MR. Hampton brings I would like to include pictures of STRONG supportive Mothers throughout History:

1. Betty Shabazz
2. Coretta Scott King
3. Afeni Shakur (my own mother)
4. Eunice Simpson
5. The Atlanta Child Murder Victm's Mothers

These Women Embody the essence of My song and I believe this would bring great substance to the video.

By all means, if you can remember any other mother's please include them

This Video Should be dedicated to

OCitA TEAL
And all of the mothers
who have lost children to
the Violence of our streets
my genuine heartfelt condolences go out to you
Tupac Shakur

Youre Consideration is
greatly Appreciated,

Tupac S

Souljah,

Everytime I read your letters it makes me smile, think, laugh and marvel at how easy it is 4 us 2 relate to one another. (And that's no hustle) It is my wish that when this letter reaches you it finds you and your family in Safety and Serenity. Now, where do I start? I'm sitting here with a fat stack of letters and through them all I immediately recognize your handwritting and know that you have finally written me back and as usual it was worth the wait. This letter is hard to write because I'm editing as I write. I'm preoccupied with having any of my statements misjudged as "hustling". ☺. First off let me answer your questions. #1 No, I don't mind long letters in fact I wish yours were longer and yes I would love to not only hear of your adventures but also share some of my own. Yes, I will write a book. Right now I'm writting 3 screenplays so upon my release I can recoup from my losses. Instead of complaining about bad movie roles or negative stereotypes I'm writing my own visions. As far as the book is concerned. I am working on doing an Autobiography but if it is at all possible I want us to do a book together. that would truly be the "BOMB"! Let me just tell you ever since I've read your book it has been going from person to person like a bible. Everybody from male inmates to female inmates have been reading it. I get a sense of pride at being the person to turn them on to your literary talents. Plus, I use your Book with the women in my life. I have asked two females to read it and we use each chapter as a door to our own lives. Like the chapter on Nikki is my favorite. I was trying over the past few months to this female in my life why it was so hard 4 me 2 trust her regardless of how Sweet & Innocent she portrayed herself to be and only after reading that chapter did she finally understand. This is some personal shit but I feel as though I can trust you so....
Okay there's that chapter where you were contimplating sharing this man with another woman. I'm in that position now. I love one woman (A) because she's dependable, loving, Supportive, And she's Young and open to me guiding her through

this crazy life (WHO AM I 2 guide?) Anyway woman "A" is from the streets and that's all she knows but I can see & feel how much she loves me. Woman "B" on the other hand is famous, rich and able to assist me financially, loving, Sensous, and very sexual. She's known me since before I got into the business and she's been there from the jump. However, she's bisexual and so into her career that we don't have much time together So I'm literally torn between an old friend who went from being of a platonic nature to a potential wife and a new friend who has been there through this whole gunshot/Rape/near death experience I have rejected them both but then reconsidered and got 'em both back. They each know of the other and I have tried to make it work as a threesome. Not sexually but committment wise. Had I not read your book I would have continued lieing & juggling with all of these other women but between them both I am completely Satisfied. I've always felt that when I love someone it is so intense that I drive them away but with "A" & "B" it evens everything out. I can satify both of them and not because I'm a "Supermanlover" but because I truly love them both and the intensity and passion I feel for them keeps me driven to please them. CAN u feel me? It's hard to explain on paper maybe when you visit me I can elaborate. which brings me to my next step. Yes I would love 4 u 2 come visit me there isn't a list but there are certain days & times for each inmate. I'll attempt to reach you by phone to make it happen. Now back to me controlling my sexual desires. Now be honest, as a woman, how could you love a man that couldn't properly satisfy you? Since men are born totally inept sexually we only learn how 2 please a woman from pleasing a woman so as rotten as it seems pratice makes perfect. Every woman I have been with has not only taken what I learned from the last woman but taught me and prepared me for the next and since I am not married and have yet to find that perfect woman you described

I am forever in search of her. I have been with many married women from wives of powerful drug lords to the wives of broke everyday Joes to the wives of quite a few very famous and rich Singers/ACTORS and seeing thier wives hungry for someone else has shown me that only by being able to completely satisfy a woman in every way, shape & form can I truly find a happy & trusting faithful relationship. Now to answer your other questions. My health is fine I truly feel blessed that other than mentally I have no scars or lasting problems from my "ordeal". I still have the complete use of every nerve, limb, and muscle and more surprisingly I can still make love and have babies after taking a shot to my scrotum! Talk about faith in GOD! :-) ! Mentally however the helpless feeling never leaves me. I can't sleep! I wake up sweaty and disorientated when I do doze off and I will never erase the faces of my attackers from my mind. 2 be honest the bulletts didn't hurt much not at first but afterwards it was painful. I didn't feel the shots to my head, hand & scrotum but because of all the muscles involved the leg wound was a real bitch! I don't really have any gun phobias meaning if it happened again I would react the same way. The pain came as I lay in the hostpital thinking about the fact that some "thug" brothers shot me. Then to hear I was found guilty of something I had not done plus wondering if my family was safe that scared me! Even with 5 gunshot wounds my paranoid ass was still sleeping with a 12 gauge and a glock. I never planned to turn myself in I planned on shooting it out but upon further reflection I realized I owed alot to my people. Although I would have been at peace, the misery of our folks would continue. Besides I'm a soldier and soldiers use strategy not emotion no matter how bad the odds!

A lot of people supported me. Jasmine Guy, Jada Pinkett, Mickey Rourke. He just wrote me funny stories. But the name that sticks out in my head the most is Tony Danza. To me he is the bomb forever. I will be his number one fan forever cuz when I got his letter I was like, "Whoa!" I was screaming to everybody.

I KNOW WHEN I WAS IN JAIL, THEY HAD A STORY ON THE NEWS—THE LOCAL NEWS OUT THERE—THAT MADONNA WAS COMING TO VISIT ME. MADONNA HAS SO MUCH POWER THAT THE GUARDS LET ME TAKE AN EXTRA SHOWER BECAUSE THEY THOUGHT SHE WAS COMING TO VISIT ME.

When I was in jail, Tyson was in jail. We would talk. He gave me some real good advice as a matter of fact.

He's given me a lot of advice. You know, I really look up to him, so for him to tell me to calm down, I was like "WHOO! It's time to calm down! If Mike Tyson is telling me that he heard about me from jail . . . calm down."

JAZ & 2PAC
Sept 2, 1995

PAC
BIG SYKE
OCT 7, 1995
DEZ
THUGZ 4 LIFE

ONE Big happy Ass family
OCT 1, 1995

June 25 1995

E5-16

May 1, 1995

Greetings Mr Welsh,

I was married on April 29, 1995 and I was given a gold wedding band. On 4/30/95 I was told to turn this wedding band over to the package room, which I did. I am now respectfully requesting my wedding band back. thank You.
My full Name is Tupac Shakur my #'s are #95A1140
I am located in E Block 5 company cell 16.

Respectfully
Yours
Tupac [signature]
(Tupac Shakur)

I'm a romantic and I thought, at the time, I wanted to be married. I got married to someone who I cared about. It was a girlfriend. I never had a girlfriend, so it was my only real girlfriend. So we just got married and it didn't work. Not because of her or me or jail. It just wasn't the right thing to do at the time. We rushed into it. When I married her, I married her for the wrong reasons.

I cared about her. But I married her because I was in jail, I was alone. I didn't want to be alone and I was like, "Well, she's there. I care about her, she cares about me, let me show some commitment." Watching *Oprah,* that's what happened. Oprah and all these shows, all these women talking about commitment, and I was like, "Oh, OK," and they was like, "Oh, it's so romantic when the guy proposes," and I was like, "Oh, OK, well, imagine if a guy's in jail and proposes."

You grow, we all grow. Either you evolve or you disappear. And I want to grow, I want to be better, you know what I mean? I want to be able to approach women, deal with women, and communicate with women and give them respect.

I was in jail. That's all I could do was watch TV, so I got married. I don't have any bad feelings toward her. We're not married anymore. There wasn't a wedding. Just in a room, justice of the peace, you do, I do, let's go.

IT WAS REAL ROMANTIC FOR A LITTLE WHILE. FOR THE MONTH THAT I WAS MARRIED. BUT IT WAS TOO YOUNG, TOO FAST. IT'S NOT TIME. AND I DIDN'T WANNA HURT HER. I CARED ABOUT HER TOO MUCH.

THE ALBUM "ME AGAINST THE WORLD"
VIBE
This is my last
interview. If I
CALVIN KLEIN JEANS

Keisha & PAC April 30 1995
STRB UP THUG LOVE 4 Life
KING & QUEEN 4 Eternity
2 MY NIGGAZ IN thugMANSION
SHIT DON'T STOP "STILL Alive in 95
Fuck them TRIX
in 96"

Thank you for my present!

Birthday
Christmas
wedding
Thanksgiving
Chanukah
Easter
Martin Luther King day
☺

Seriously – I really appreciate it. I truly have the best husband in the whole wide world!

You get time to appreciate things. Perspective. You start looking at things differently, like everything's not so important. You don't take things so personally.

JAIL WILL DO THAT FOR YOU, BECAUSE YOU TALKING TO KILLERS AND IF THEY SAY SOMETHING YOU DON'T LIKE, YOU CAN'T BE LIKE, "WHAT?" YOU GOT TO BE LIKE, "OK, LOOK MAN, WOULD YOU MIND NOT CALLING ME . . . " YOU KNOW WHAT I MEAN? ANGER MANAGEMENT, LIKE A MO. GUARDS PUSHING YOU, CALLIN' YOU NAMES, TELLING YOU TO HURRY UP, GET OUT OF THE SHOWER. YOU CAN'T SAY, "WHAT, I'M TAKING A SHOWER!" YOU GOTTA BE LIKE, "YES, SIR." SO I LEARNED THAT—HUMILITY. I THINK BEING HUMBLE IS GOOD. YOU GET TO SEE THINGS MORE. AND I GOT THAT FROM BEING IN JAIL WHERE YOU DON'T TALK SO MUCH.

Everyone changes, become better people. We all should get that chance. I just want my chance.

2 Be Read Aloud At next family meeting.

My Dearest family,

Well as U all Know when niggaz get locked up they are forced 2 do alot of thinking and planning. Thier futures become clear as day when thought about over and over again. Anyway since i don't talk much 2 everyone i will attempt to communicate through this letter please hear me out and bare with me. First of all I give much respect to our elders: Tom, Jean, Afeni, Helena, Ignae, and Yassmyn. but allow me to do what I feel must be done 2 preserve our family. First off, due 2 some unfortunate blow of misfortune our woman have had the duty of raising us all and in thier journey they have made mistakes but all in all they have done a good job with what was against them Tom has served as a father figure 4 alot of us and by no means am i trying 2 deny this, however we have come to the point where the next generation has to do our share. More importantly the men. By men i mean; Myself, Billy, Scott, Kenny, and Gary. It is time we do what must be done to keep our family not only together but prosperous. Unfortunately, I am broke and obviously in the pen so I am no longer able 2 make due on all the promises i had 4 us but we still can make it. I propose we all collectively invest in a family Resturant and put in some hardwork. Here's the plan

The Atmospere will be old blues & Soul Jams we'll have a Jukebox and a water fountain dispenser. The walls will have platinums and photos of famous people & Newsclippings of mine & my Mom's & Katari Little league flix. Baby Pictures & plants (Jean can pick 'em) Jean, Ma, Ignae, & Helena in the Kitchen cooking. Tom, billy, [illegible] & G deliveries. Kenny, Jamala, Mailing Hostess & Host. Mailing, Malcolm (cashiers) [illegible], [illegible], Sekyina, Shona & Dina Waiters & Waitress. Nelson, Katari, & Motaw busboys & dishes. we call it "AROUND THE WAY CAFE" what do u think? well we need 2 do Some research to find out how much we need & what we need. Watani can probably be of Some help. Now the next thing is deeper in order for us to be as strong as we can be we have to let go of the negative chains that got us. No More interfamily fucking. If u Say we cousins then we cousins no fucking. No getting high in front of the babiez. No more children in grown folks conversations. No more serets. Everybody should be responsible to the family first & themselves Second We are all we got. the elders have to also be more cognizant of our problems and advise us of better routes. No More ghetto shit let's take it 2 the next level. Also stop Smiling in each other faces when u know u doing Some foul shit. Be honest with each other We all make mistakes but one person's secret could destroy us all. Please yall let's do this cafe thing let's get tight

let's have more control over our destinies. by the time y'all get this me & Keisha will have gotten married and when i finally settle down I plan on living in Pheonix w/ my wife but I can't do it until we are Solid and everybody's on their feet. This resturant will do it. So everybody do thier best. Don't just forget what I said cuz I took my time 2 write this at least do the research. Don't get too sidetracked. I have big dreams 4 us but we need discipline and a sense of respect 4 each other. Our men put thier lives out daily 2 represent our females so please give us respect 4 as long as we are worthy of it. Our women are our Hope & future let's be more respectful & watchful 4 them. Mailing will be coming through soon to reinforce Some of this. We are going to make it but it has to be "We" not "Me". Every sucessful family has a head of the family and I want to have that responsibility & honor. I love u all and I want to do this. I will need wise counsel I nominate Tom, Jean, Afeni, Helena, & Ignae (Louisa, Yas, & Mootaw's fam are honorary counsel) a counsel of elders 2 guide me. A LT. (Billy) [illegible] Souljah's (Katari, Malcolm, Zayd, Mootaw, Kenny, G & Scott) and for our youth & our unit we need guidance, Support and understanding. This will be (Mailing, Jamala, Sekyina, Dina, Shona, Nelson, Mutulu, Moepreme, Geronimo etc)

We pool our funds together, beg, borrow & steal and purchase a worthy location (either buy or rent) Then we clean, rebuild and decorate the place to be A family atmosphere. Get a permit and whatever other documents and build us a sit down/Take out home cooked Soulfood & Cultural Plates Resturant. Here's a Sample menu

Glo's Fried chicken Dinner
2PAC's Barb B Q chicken Dinner
Ignae's GUMBO
Kenny's Fried Fish dinner
Imani & Zinga's Peppersteak with Rice
Helena & Louisa's Barb B Q Beef
Billy's Meatloaf
FAY's Dominican Chicken & Rice
Katari & Alu's Curry goat Dinner
Scott's curry chicken DINNER
Nelson's & Malcolm's Spagetti & Meatballs dinner
Sekyina's Lasagna Dinner
Jamala's Fried Jumbo Shrimp dinner
Tom's T.C. Burger
Dina & Shona's cheeseburger
Gary's All day Breakfast (2 eggs bacon or Sausage, Pancakes & grits)

Vege's: Macaroni & cheese, greens, redbeans & rice, potato Salad & cabbage

Plus Celebrity Dishes like Jada Pinkett's Vege Platter Jasmine Guy's grilled cheese YoYo's French Fries etc!

Jamala - starting speaking real clear with Imani read 2 her & be attentive. Do your best help research for the family resturant. Keep it together. Russell can wait we need u Boo!

That's All
whoever
I missed
I'll get later
it's late
C ya soon
heed to this
pay y'All!

Love
YA Peoples
[signature]

West Up Playa!

yeh, yeh, it's been awhile since I last reached out 2 U but a nigga been maintaining here in these cells, cages & bars. U know can't nuthin stop me but loss of breath and I'm still breathing so it's still on. I've been making hella movez though I'm spittin at Suge at Deathrow about merging my shit with thiers. I aint sure though. I told them 3 albulms 3 years and 6 million yes or no. So I'm waiting on that move

Bangsta, (LT.)

I didn't get the cigz & magazines because u didn't send them closed & wrapped from a vendor. But I sent them to Keisha. Try again. Yo! I'll C U soon so I'll hold my words til then this letter is because I got this in the mail (the letter enclosed) and I want u 2 investigate it.

STAY UP

Thug Love 2 the fullest

from

DA

Duece

It can't stop! Won't stop thug 4 Life!

~~Biggie~~ ~~Puffy~~ ~~Lil Shawn~~ ~~Jimmy~~ ~~Jack~~ ~~Rick~~

~~Andre~~ ~~Craig Mack~~ ~~Badboy~~ ~~Tut~~ ~~Stretch~~

I BEEN JAILED DOWN FOR ELEVEN MONTHS. I'M VULNERABLE. STUCK IN MY CELL. THIS HERE LIFESTYLE, THIS IS HARD.

I KNEW I COULD TRUST NOBODY. TRUST NO-BO-DY.

Straight up, my closet friends did me in. My closet friends, my homies, people I would have took care of their whole family, I would took care of everything for them, I would have looked out for them, put them in the game, turned on me. Fear is stronger than love. Remember that. Fear is stronger than love. All the love I gave did me nothing when it came to fear. So it is all good. I am a soldier and I will always survive.

I WILL CONSTANTLY COME BACK. THE ONLY THING THAT CAN KILL ME IS DEATH.

WHEN I WAS IN JAIL, THEY TOOK MY PIECE OFF THE BOARD SO I CAN'T PLAY NO MORE. NOW I'M BACK ON THE BOARD, I'M BACK TO BEING A CHESS PLAYER. EVERY MOVE THAT I MAKE, SOMETHING IS GONNA GO ALONG WITH THAT, THERE'S GONNA BE A RESPONSE. IT WAS LIKE, "OK, YOU READY, PAC?" THIS IS GONNA BE THE CHESS GAME, NOW IT'S A CHESS GAME.

2.25 refundable from gross sales of 3 albulms
you may get refunded from first profit.
but due upon signing
1 million advance for 3 albulms unrefundable
and due upon signing

1.5 million for publishing. 500,000 due upon recieving
~~receipt of~~ "R U STILL down" 500,000 due upon
completion of "America's Euthanasia", 500,000 due
upun recieving "Untitled final Album".

for ~~Tupac~~ "2PAC" contract the total is 4.75 million for 3 albums
2.25 refundable
with "Live 2 tell" add 1 million
and option to get first choice at
future scripts and books.

Before I can sign these things must be included
and the proper changes must be made
the option clause must be Voluntary.

Sept. 15, 1995

TO: INTERSCOPE RECORDS

FROM: TUPAC SHAKUR

RE: AUTHORIZATION TO REPRESENT TUPAC SHAKUR

THIS MEMO WILL CONFIRM THAT SUGE KNIGHT & DAVID KENNER ARE THE ONLY PEOPLE AUTHORIZED TO REPRESENT ME IN CONNECTION WITH MY MUSIC AND RECORDING. SUGE KNIGHT IS MY MANAGER AND DAVID KENNER MY LAWYER FOR THESE PURPOSES.

DATED: September 16, 1995 [signature] TUPAC SHAKUR

B 41

SEPT 15, 1995

SUGE KNIGHT IS TO BE MY MANAGER FOR ALL MUSIC ENDEVERS FOR A PERIOD OF THREE YEARS. SUGE WILL CAUSE A CONTRACT TO BE ENTERED INTO BY AND BETWEEN TUPAC SHAKUR AND DEATH ROW RECORDS WHICH WILL INCLUDE THE FOLLOWING DEAL POINTS:

ALBUM ONE:

1. TO BE RELEASED IN 1995. ALBUM TO CONSIST OF ALREADY RECORDED MATERIAL TO BE REMIXED BY DR. DRE. SNOOP DOGGY DOGG SHALL MAKE A GUEST APPEARANCE ON SAID ALBUM.

2. TUPAC SHALL RECEIVE THE FOLLOWING ADVANCES:
   - A. ONE MILLION UPON EXECUTION OF DOCUMENTS
   - B 125,000 FOR PURCHASE OF CAR
   - C. 120,000 EXPENSE ALLOWANCE FOR 12 MONTHS

SK

A 28

- D. 250,000 LEGAL FUND ~~FEE~~ TO BE SPENT THROUGH CHALETREE AT THE DIRECTION OF TUPAC
- E. DEATH ROW SHALL SECURE THE SERVICES OF DAVID KENNER TO HANDLE TUPAC'S LOS ANGELES CASES.

3. TUPAC SHALL RECEIVE 18 POINTS WITH ONE POINT BUMPS AT GOLD AND PLATINUM.

ALBUM TWO

TO BE RELEASED IN 1996 T.S.

1. 18 POINTS - 1 POINT BUMP AT GOLD AND PLATINUM

2. 1 MILLION ADVANCE (ALL IN) FOR EVERY MILLION RECORDS SOLD ON ALBUM ONE.

ALBUM THREE

TO BE RELEASED IN 1997 T.S. SK

1. 18 POINTS - 1 POINT BUMP AT GOLD AND PLATINUM.

2. ADV OF 1 MILLION (ALL IN) FOR

EVERY MILLION RECORDS SOLD ON ALBUM TWO.

DATED: September 16, 1995 [signature] TUPAC SHAKUR

DATED: 9-15-95 [signature] SUGE KNIGHT

Sept 25, 1995

Peace Chuck

First of all, I'm sure u Know how highly respected & loved u R by me so your letter definitely warmed my heart. I was also touched by your offer and show of support. It will not go unnoticed. Thankx! It was good 2 hear how well u are doing but hey it's only right. Back in the dayz, on tour with u I learned so much from what u did and how u did it. It may be hard 2 c but u have alwayz played a major role in what it is I do 2day. I have a program I want 2 put together and I would like 4 U 2 be a part of it. I'll explain it 2 U in detail on another occassion. I also have a part 4 U in this movie if u R willing and 2 push my luck even more I would be honored if u would appear on this track 4 my next album "Euthanasia" the track is called "Da Struggle Continuez" it will also feature Sista Souljah if God wills. So let me Know. I just recieved word that my bail pending appeal has been granted so I should be free by the time u recieve this. I'll include a number of my assistant until I get settled. I just signed 2 Deathrow so I should be working on this album soon. Thanx again Chuck! I do believe we can make a difference and I have every intention of doing just that. STAY STRONG!. Keep me in

your heart & let'z continue 2 offer & inspire
~~stiff~~ Resistance. I Remain

Eternal

[signature]

Da Struggle Continuez!

201 509 Yaasmyn Fula

- it's either 509

or

sorry! ☺

Reach Out 4 me
Soldier!

and if & when u need me
call me,
I'm there!

DEATH ROW 1995–1996

IT'S NOT A VIOLENT WAR, BUT IT'S A WAR.

Suddenly, I was out on bail pending my appeal. The way that the criminal justice system works is that when you're convicted, you have a chance to appeal. And while you appeal, you can be out on bail. If I win my appeal—which if God wills, I will—I will have done eleven months for nothing.

I WAS RELIEVED, HAPPY TO BE HOME. IT'S A TRIP WHEN YOU KNOW THAT LAST WEEK YOU WERE IN JAIL. I WAS IN THIS LITTLE CELL, IT WAS REAL DIRTY, NOT HAVING ANY HOT WATER, DUDES WAS TELLING ME WHEN TO SHOWER, WHEN TO EAT AND ALL THAT. AND THE NEXT WEEK I'M UP IN MONTY'S WITH CRISTAL CHAMPAGNE, FILET MIGNON, LOBSTER AND SHRIMPS.

Everybody kept going, "Come on, let me take you out, let me take you out. Oh you ain't eat? You home? Oh come on, let me take you to dinner." I had four breakfast celebrations and everything. We was all up in Roscoe's. I even celebrated at El Polo Loco. We had a celebration up in there cuz I was dreaming about El Polo Loco the whole time. I was like, I can't wait to get out. I'm going straight to L.A., I'm going straight to El Polo Loco. Then I'm going here, then I'm going here.

THEN I WANTED TO DRIVE UP AND DOWN SUNSET. BECAUSE I LOVE L.A.—WITH A PASSION. I LOVE SUNSET. I LOVE EVERYTHING ABOUT L.A. AND I JUST WANTED TO DRIVE UP AND DOWN THERE AND LOOK AT THE SIGNS AND THE PEOPLE. YOU KNOW, THE ENERGY—THAT'S L.A.

MOSCHINO

The Secretary of State
of the United States of America
hereby requests all whom it may concern to permit the citizen/
national of the United States named herein to pass
without delay or hindrance and in case of need to
give all lawful aid and protection.

Le Secrétaire d'Etat
des Etats-Unis d'Amérique
prie par les présentes toutes autorités compétentes de laisser passer
le citoyen ou ressortissant des Etats-Unis titulaire du présent passeport,
sans délai ni difficulté et, en cas de besoin, de lui accorder
toute aide et protection légitimes.

SIGNATURE OF BEARER/SIGNATURE DU TITULAIRE

NOT VALID UNTIL SIGNED

UNITED STATES OF AMERICA

PASSPORT
PASSEPORT
USA

Type/Catégorie: P
Code of issuing State / code du pays émetteur: USA
PASSPORT NO./NO. DU PASSEPORT: 035635027

Surname / Nom: SHAKUR

Given names / Prénoms: TUPAC AMARU

Nationality / Nationalité: UNITED STATES OF AMERICA

Date of birth / Date de naissance: 16 JUN/JUN 71

Sex / Sexe: M
Place of birth / Lieu de naissance: NEW YORK, U.S.A.

Date of issue / Date de délivrance: 08 DEC/DEC 95
Date of expiration / Date d'expiration: 07 DEC/DEC 05

Authority / Autorité: PASSPORT AGENCY LOS ANGELES

Amendments/ Modifications SEE PAGE 24

P<USASHAKUR<<TUPAC<AMARU<<<<<<<<<<<<<<<<<<<<

0356350273USA7106163M0512077<<<<<<<<<<<<<<<4

I BELIEVE THAT I'M A NATURAL BORN LEADER. I CAN TAKE ORDERS CUZ I'M A GOOD SOLDIER, BUT I LIKE TO GIVE ORDERS, LIKE TO FOLLOW MY OWN HEART.

I do what I gotta do to get to the front seat. I work hard. I gotta be involved, I gotta excel at it. It can't be a small thing, it gotta be a big thing.

I ONLY WROTE ONE SONG IN JAIL. I COULDN'T WRITE. BUT THE DAY I GOT OUT, WHEN I GOT OUT, IN THE STUDIO, I HAD WRITTEN TWENTY SONGS IN LESS THAN TWO WEEKS. SO THAT'S WHEN IT ALL CAME OUT. FREEDOM, INSPIRATION.

1 enter the center in the mind of sinner
fragmented thoughtz of criminal preoccuppied with winner
2 missin the pieces of his mind turnin his thoughtz 2 crymes
Random shotz rang blind these r designz of an angry mind
3 where they find me In these Dangerouz Timez
Ride so Homicidez Ratez I'm a break each time
4 Makavelli was the Name i chose when i strategize
enemiez die multiply my crimez
5 When sippin hennessey my venom is Deadly them Bad Boyz ain't ready
he died lookin at me shooked as hell
6 Picture me growin i save this tortured brain
I put this shit inside ~~my~~ ya armz let it torch ya veinz
7 Visionz! of Better livin or prison is secondary
Never 2 be seen my ~~Murder~~ whole team is legendary
8 a crew of crooked individualz laced with criminal mindz
* How do we survive in these crymanal timez

Az Made Niggaz

think of the sacrice the price we paid
Throughout these criminal timez count all the livez we gave
started out stolen sold as a slave figure
But now we M.O.B.

CAME OUT OF JAIL, WENT STRAIGHT TO THE STUDIO. AND I DID TWENTY-FOUR TRACKS. IT'S A DOUBLE ALBUM CALLED *ALL EYEZ ON ME*. IT'S JUST A GIFT FOR MY FANS THAT SUPPORTED ME WHILE I WAS LOCKED DOWN.

I got a lot of letters, lot of support. Plus I had so much to say I figured this would be the best way to vent it instead of paying some psychotherapist like, $50 million. I just went in the studio. It's cheaper.

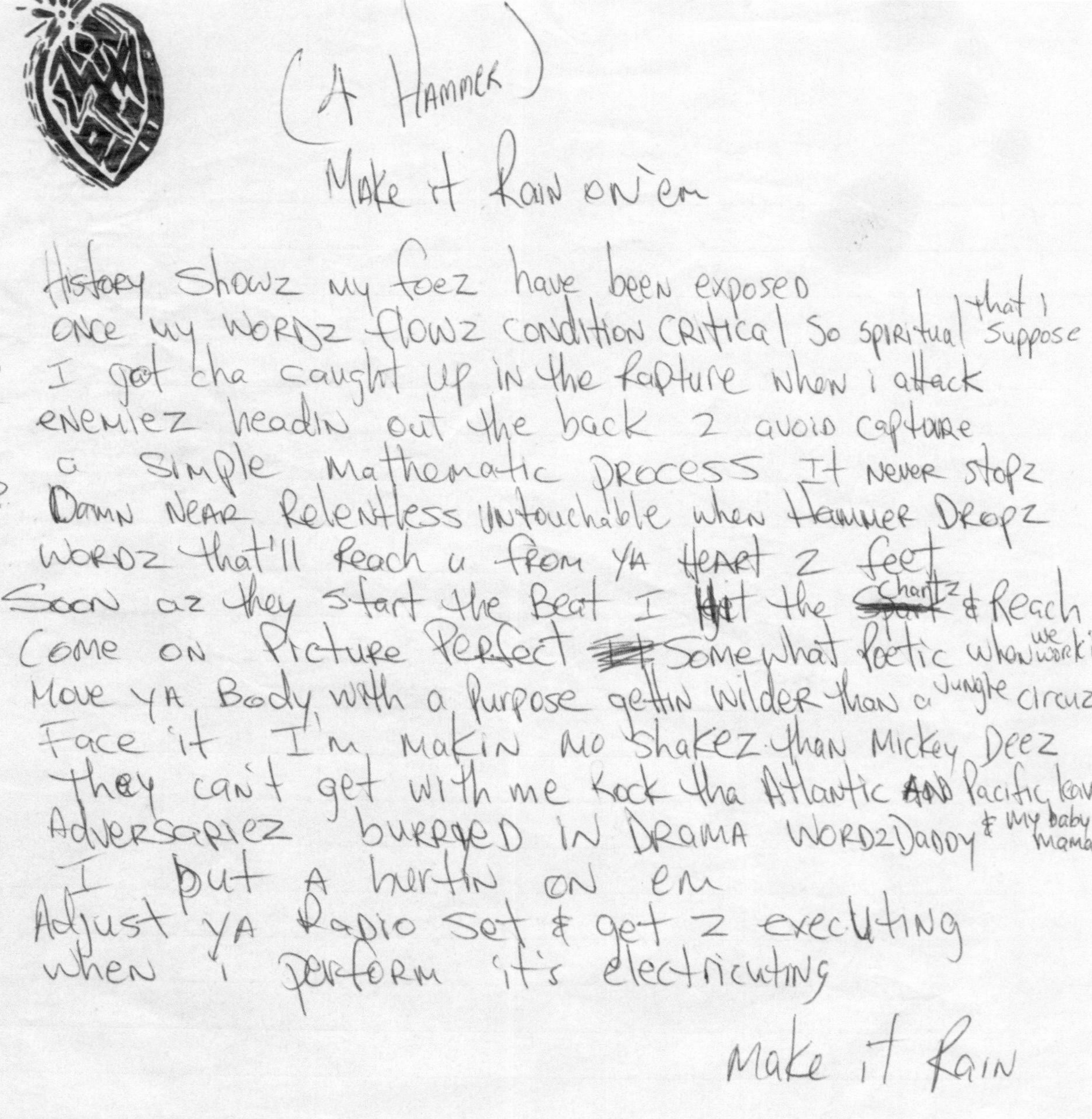

(A Hammer)

Make it Rain on'em

1 History showz my foez have been exposed
once my wordz flowz condition critical so spiritual that i suppose
2 I got cha caught up in the rapture when i attack
enemiez headin out the back 2 avoid capture
3 a simple mathematic process it never stopz
Damn near relentless untouchable when Hammer Dropz
4 wordz that'll reach u from ya heart 2 feet
Soon az they start the beat I hit the ~~spot~~ chartz & reach
5 Come on picture perfect ~~it~~ somewhat poetic when we work it
Move ya body with a purpose gettin wilder than a jungle circuz
6 Face it I'm makin mo shakez than Mickey Deez
they can't get with me rock tha Atlantic ~~and~~ pacific leave
7 Adversariez burried in drama wordz 2 daddy & my baby mama
I put a hurtin on em
8 Adjust ya radio set & get 2 executing
when i perform it's electricuting

Make it Rain

I'll take away the Rain ~~How~~ & Make it Rain

California Love! w/Dre & Roger

Duck what u screamin I'm California dreamin
the land of Angelz & Gangbangaz Earthquakez & demonz
come take a ride 2 the west side
I love L.A. cuz here we play and all the rest try
the best die peep out the home of skanless

Now it's a job. Before, I didn't know I was working. I didn't know you work all day everyday, twenty-four hours. I thought, I'm not doing a movie, I'm just famous. I don't have to do anything. But you work everyday, all day. You have to work on how you treat people, what image you have, what you do around people, and now I work. I believe I'm more responsible, more mature, more focused. And I will be even more focused, more responsible, more mature in time.

IN *VIBE* I WAS LIKE, "I'M NOT RAPPIN' NO MORE," BECAUSE I COULDN'T REMEMBER WHY I WAS RAPPIN'. WHY SHOULD I DO IT, IF YOU GOT THE GROUPIES, THE LIES, THE MEDIA, THE CHARGES, THE LAWSUITS? BUT THEN WHEN I WAS IN JAIL, I WAS AWAY FROM IT FOR SO LONG I WAS LIKE, I REALLY LIKE GOING INTO THE STUDIO, I REALLY LIKE CREATING. I REALLY LIKE HEARING MY SONG ON THE RADIO. YOU KNOW, I LIKE MUSIC, AND I LIKE ACTING. I LIKE DOING IT.

Death Row is a successful record company. It runs efficiently. Everything they've released has sold in excess of four million copies. I'm saying, why not be there? I really like everybody on the record company. I like Suge. That's my homie. I like Snoop, Dre, and Nate, and all them. I hang out with them anyway, so now it's just official. Suge ain't no gangster, man. He's chillin'.

Me comin' to Death Row, one of the main reasons besides Suge was Snoop. The man's got so much style. I felt like since me and Snoop's music was often coupled together when we were being criticized and when we were being praised, we getting, you know, sales and all that. So I said it would be a wise decision to team up with them and make this allegiance that much more stronger, and the vibe coming out the West Coast scene that much more heavier.

I'M A SUPER POWER. DEATH ROW IS A SUPER POWER. LET'S COMBINE SUPER POWERS AND ALLY, AND REALLY HIT 'EM. AND THAT'S ONE OF THE BIGGEST COMBINATIONS YOU CAN GET.

Ma' Babiez Mama

By 2Pac

1 Aint Nothin ~~Really~~ Changed At least 4 me My feelingz still the Same
We been together 2 long 2 be involved in childish game
Although At timez u Nag being with u is Really not that bad
We Reminisse and get 2 trippin off the fightz we had
3 ~~Remember~~ we went bustin all my windowz stealin all my indo u
Catchin Me with old hoez cuttin up my New clothz
4 Shavin my head with a Razor givin me Massagez
Even though u stole my heart I aint the type 2 press chargez
5 It's a sticky situation ~~all~~ the Drama I be facin
Trying 2 take my baby Mama on a fantasy vacation
6 While I'm Snatchin & taking I'll be Stackin what I'm makin
Caz u Know my Kidz need transportation
7 I hate 2 C u walkin at the train station
Walkin' in puddlez that the drizzlin Rain makin'
8 And Even though my Momz hate u and yo Momz Can't stand me
Don't even trip we got our family

Ma Baby Mama

2 of Amerikaz Mozt Wanted
Video Treatment

Ext opening Scene: night time
Snoop'z private jet shows up at airport Snoop exitz with his 2 exotic female body guardz. He jumps in Rolls and pulls off in hurry

Int Rolls -
Snoop on cellular frantically calling ...

Int. Pac sits at a conference table with ~~a well dressed white man~~ [crossed out] [crossed out lines]

Syke standz by Door with bogart. Phone Ringz
Syke Answerz and sayz

Syke!
it's Dogg! He sayz it's important that he speakz 2 u and only u.

Pac!
whatz up Homie

Sherise
44 171
RM 640

I MEAN TO ME, I KNOW WHAT GOOD MORALS ARE. IT WOULD SEEM YOU'RE SUPPOSED TO DISREGARD GOOD MORALS WHEN YOU'RE LIVING IN A CRAZY BAD WORLD. IF YOU'RE LIVING CURSED, HOW CAN YOU LIVE LIKE AN ANGEL? IF YOU'RE IN HELL, HOW CAN YOU LIVE LIKE AN ANGEL? YOU'RE SURROUNDED BY DEVILS AND YOU'RE SUPPOSED TO LIVE LIKE AN ANGEL. THAT'S LIKE SUICIDE, YOU KNOW WHAT I'M SAYIN'?

I HAVE LOVE FOR EVERYBODY.

Free Geronimo Pratt...
AND ALL
Political Prisoners
FREE

I USUALLY MESS UP, BUT I LEARN. I COME BACK STRONGER. EVERYONE CHANGES, BECOMES BETTER PEOPLE. WE ALL SHOULD GET THAT CHANCE. I JUST WANT MY CHANCE.

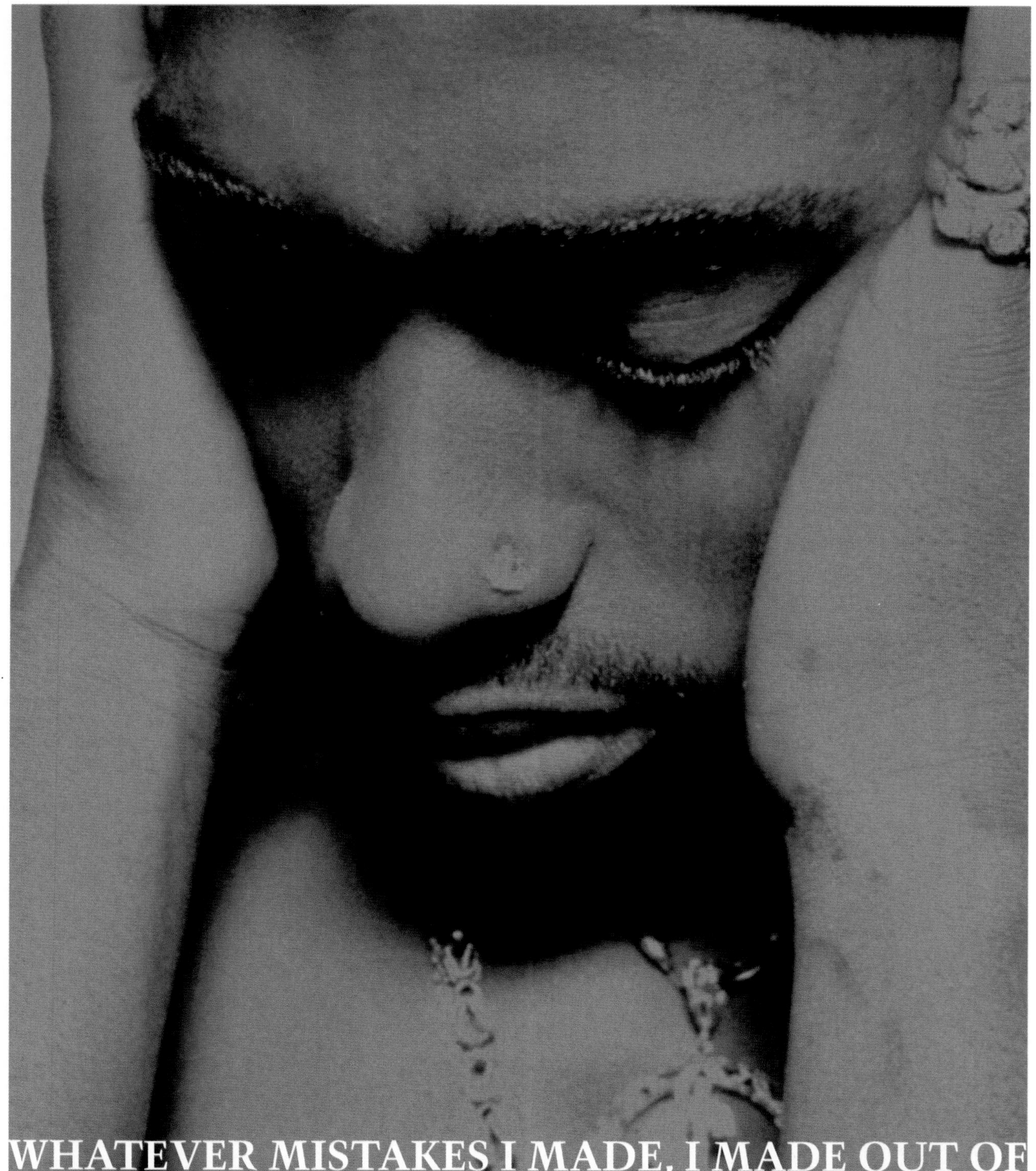

WHATEVER MISTAKES I MADE, I MADE OUT OF IGNORANCE, NOT OUT OF DISRESPECT. I WAS A REACTIONARY. NOW I DON'T DO THAT ANYMORE. SAME PERSON, JUST I DON'T REACT. BEFORE, I REACTED. I DIDN'T LIKE THE CAMERAS.

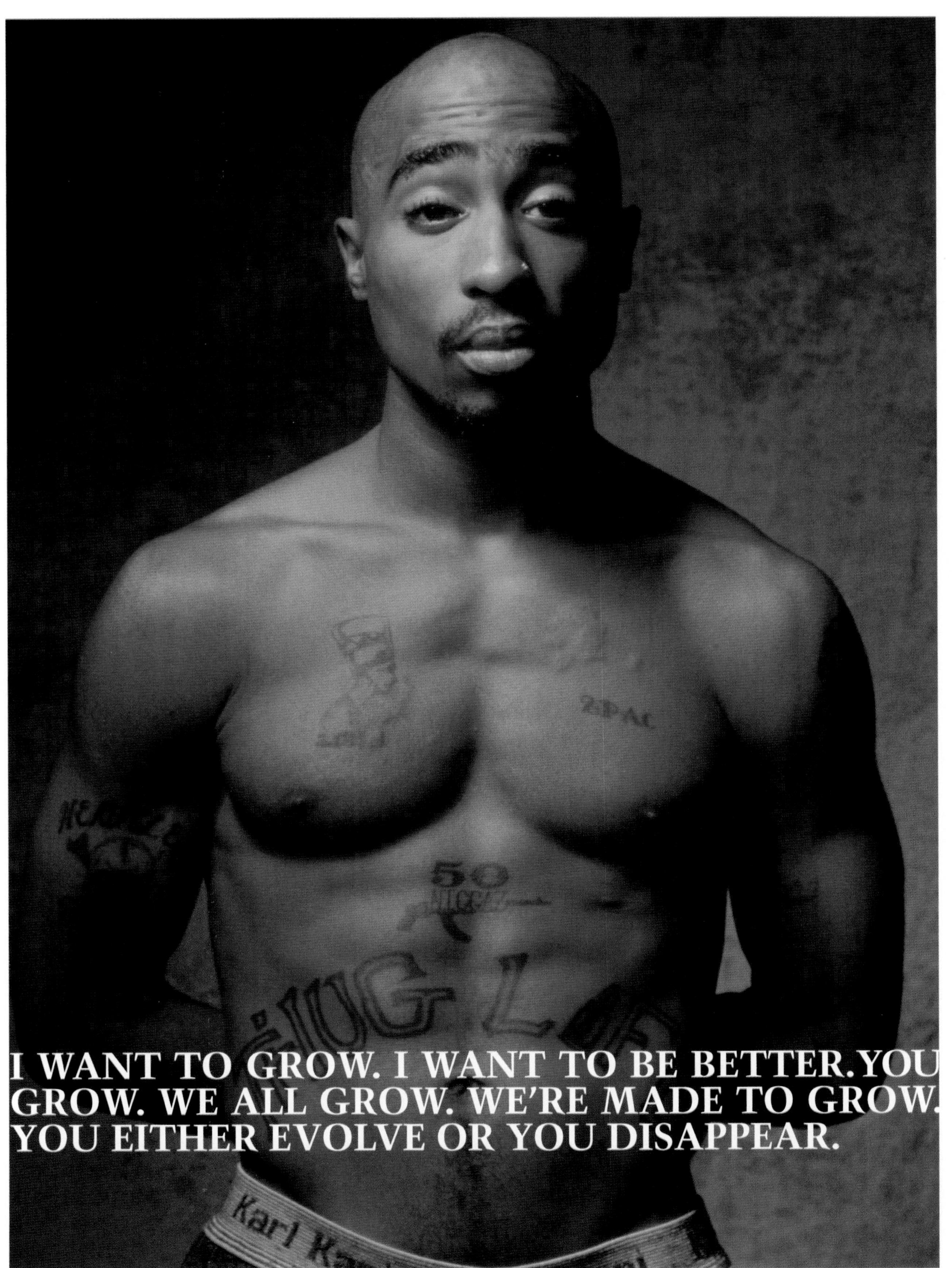
I WANT TO GROW. I WANT TO BE BETTER. YOU GROW. WE ALL GROW. WE'RE MADE TO GROW. YOU EITHER EVOLVE OR YOU DISAPPEAR.

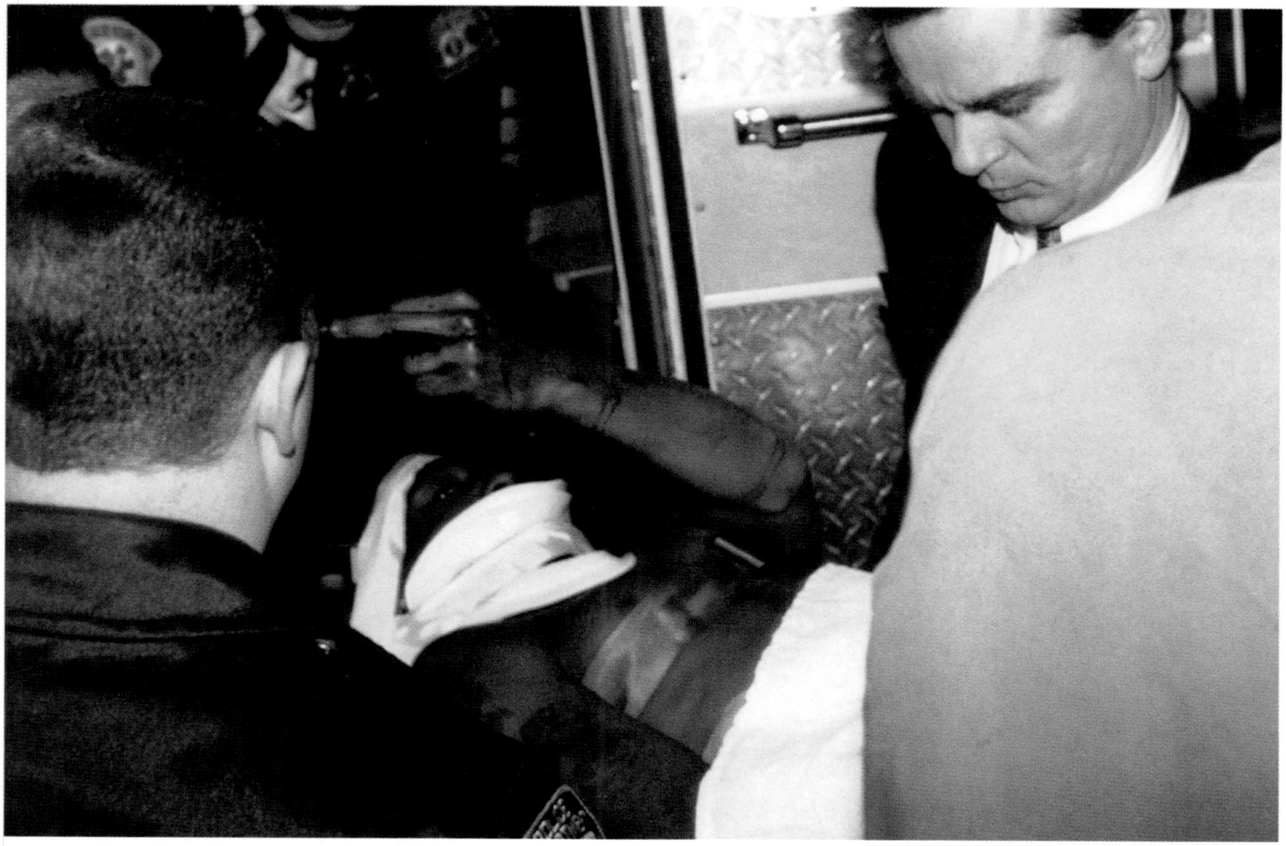

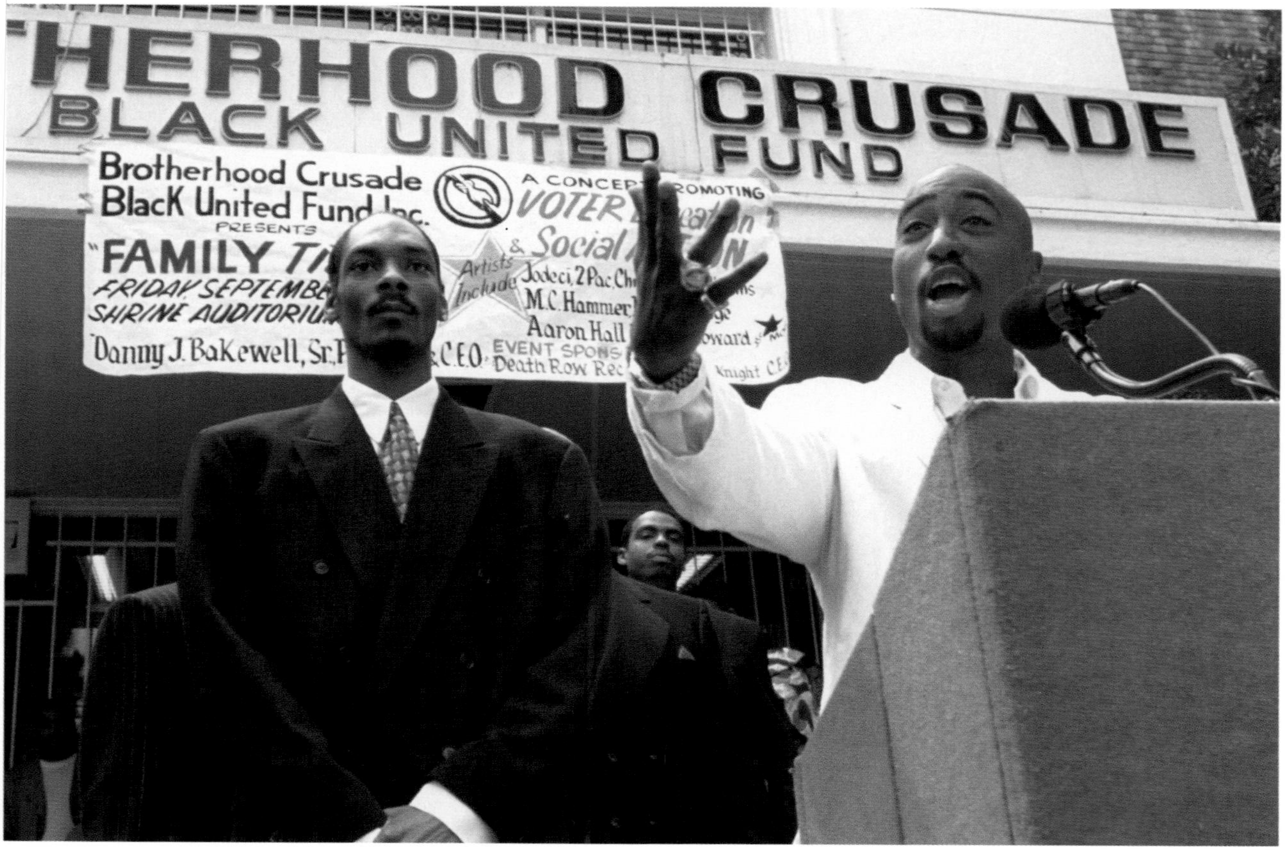
HERHOOD CRUSADE
BLACK UNITED FUND
Brotherhood Crusade
Black United Fund Inc.
PRESENTS
"FAMILY
Artists Include
M.C. Hammer
Aaron Hall
Danny J. BaKewell, Sr.
Death Row Rec

MACLORD

I WANT TO BE IN THE FUTURE KNOWN AS SOMEBODY. I WANT PEOPLE TO BE TALKING ABOUT ME LIKE, *REMEMBER WHEN HE WAS REAL BAD?*

I STILL GET LOVE FROM MY COMMUNITY. I CAN STILL GO DOWN THE STREET, RIDE PAST A CROWD AND THEY SCREAM, YOU KNOW? IT'S LIKE I OWE THEM EVERYTHING, THAT'S WHERE I OWE EVERYTHING—TO THE HOOD.

I got love there. I got love from thugs, from street dudes. We can do anything if you just give us a shot and stop trying to beat us down. We need to be in control of ourselves.

I AIN'T SCARED, YOU KNOW WHAT I'M SAYIN'? THERE'S DEATH AND LIFE, AND THERE IS NO LIFE IF YOU AIN'T FIGHTING.

Timberland
THUG LIFE

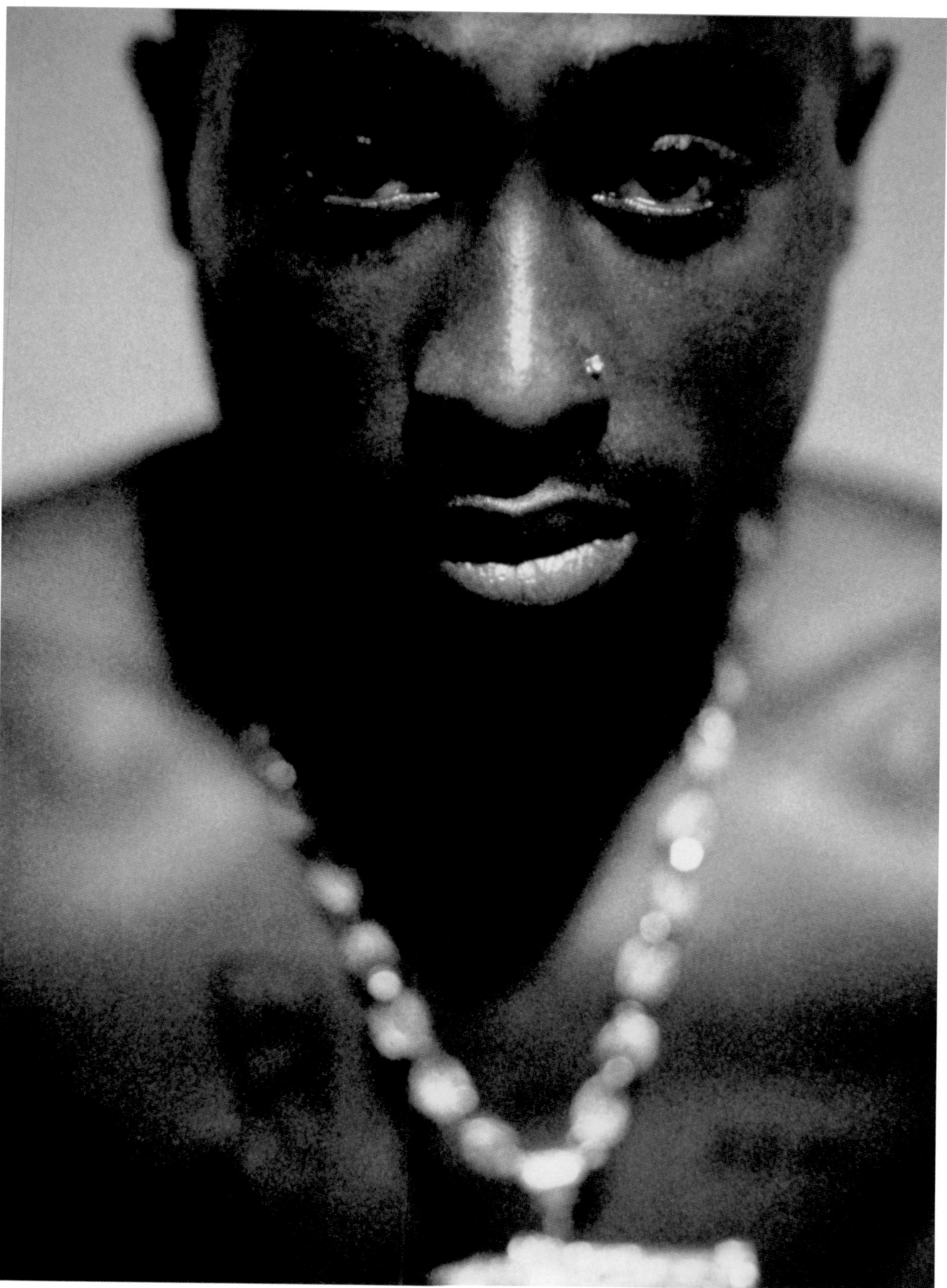

Hard 2 Kill verse III

Don't Pay Attention 2 My Pain
1 ~~2 whom it may concern~~ Don't follow me I'm lost
On the Newz getting cruciffed hanging from a cross
2 all my homiez from my background
wanna stab me in the back cuz I Rap now
3 I aint never turned back it's a Ratrace
and u a target if u strapped with a blackface
4 and I've been labeled as a threat 2 Society kill me where I stand
Just A ghetto boy trying 2 a motherfukin man
5 if I'm wrong send me 2 my maker in a casket
2 keep from getting my ass kicked niggaz got blasted
6 I didn't mean 2 kill em but the coward try 2 do me
Put 2 bulletz in his dome like the moviez
7 and kept on slept on and tired of being stepon
it's him or me so I fired & I kept going
8 my mama told me leave so I left
cops on my tail so I bail til I'm outta breath
9 What's left of my life but misery
wanna c me bleed cuz yall aint real as me
10 But I'm a leave 'em how I came
every nigga in the game know my motherfuking name
11 B4 I leave hit the weed then I breathe my last breath
keep swingin til my death

I'm hard 2 kill

When Nobody Lovez Me

1 get in my ride bump a oldiez tape
it's Time 2 ride Alone cuz Phony Homiez iz fake
2 Niggaz change like the weather supposed 2 be forever
cuz of Money Niggaz aint even together
3 what i c is simple greed cuz this industry
will make a honest man change turn 2 deciet
4 fuck it! I gotta be a Man only way 2 learn is 2 try
Take my chances until i get my turn in a fly
5 where I'm headin aint no adversariez
u get 2 hook up with the homiez that u haven't burried
6 Don't be worried Aint no gun shotz or punk copz
this our block
Hook up the mic when i recite witness a crowd flock
7 probably a dreamer but it seemz as clear as the thingz
everybody wishes in the mind but nothin has changed
8 sick of the Pressure being blamed 4 Hell
until it change I remain in my cell

when nobody love me

Knocking On ~~Heaven's~~ Door

~~Scared Man Can't Win~~ Remember Me

1 perhaps i was blind 2 the facts Stabbed in the back
I couldn't trust my own homiez Just a bunch of Dirty ratz
2 Will i Succeed paranoid from the weed
Hocus Pocus try 2 focus but i cant see
3 In my mind a blind man doing time
~~What's my~~ [Look 2 my] future cuz my Past is all behind me
4 Is it crime 2 Fight 4 what is mine
everybody dieing [tell me] what's the use in trying,
5 I've been trapped since birth Cautious cuz I'm cursed
fantasiez of my family in a hearse
6 And they Say it's the White Man I should fear
but it's my own Kind Doing all the Killing here
7 I can't lie Aint no love 4 the other side
Jealousy inside Make 'em wish I ~~mother fuka~~ Died
8 And My Lord tell me what im living 4
everybody's dropping got me Knocking on Heaven's Door
9 So Many enemiez Dreamed of Killing Me
If these the killing fields then ~~S... heaven weed~~ [I'm the growing] seed
10 All My Memoriez Seeing Brothaz Bleed
And everybody grieves But still Nobody Sees
11 Recollect your thought Don't get caught up in the MIX
cuz the media is full of dirty trix

Remember Me

still i aint dead yet

RahRah 987 7760

Dear mama don't cry
Your baby boy's doin' good
Tell the homies I'm in heaven and it ain't got hoods
Seen a show with Marvin Gaye last night
It had me shook
Drinking peppermint schnapps with Jackie Wilson
And Sam Cooke
Then some lady named Billie Holiday sang
Sittin' there kickin' it with Malcolm till the day came
Lil' Latasha sure grown
Tell the lady in the liquor store that she's forgiven
So come home
Maybe in time you'll understand
Only God can save us
Where Miles Davis cutting loose with the band
Just think of all the people that you knew in the past that passed on
They in heaven found peace at last
Picture a place that they exist together
There has to be a place better than this
In Heaven
So right before I sleep dear God what I'm askin'
Remember this face save me a place
In Thugz Mansion

Note from Afeni Shakur

Tupac loved to read! Books were a constant part of his life. As much as Tupac loved to read, he enjoyed talking.

From our earliest commitment to a documentary of Tupac Shakur's life, we had to allow Tupac to narrate his own journey through film. The embryo of this important book was already beginning to impose itself upon our production plans for the film. It was as if Tupac's spirit reminded us that he wanted to tell his own story not only on film, but in print. The film is a very powerful voice for Tupac, but an accompanying book was obviously unavoidable. Amaru's own Ms. Karolyn Ali went searching for publishers who would not distort our vision for this project. Thankfully, we did not have to search further than Judith Curr, who published Tupac's *The Rose That Grew from Concrete*. When Judith took over the helm at Atria, we became reenergized with her faith in our project.

This book is a result of the work of many people. More importantly, the book is an extension of my son's thoughts, beliefs, and the way he viewed life! Thank you, Tupac, for sharing your world on film and in the pages of this book. We hope you are not disappointed.

Love,

Mom

Captions: Page 4 Afeni Shakur at Black Panther press conference, 1971; Page 5 (l) Afeni at poetry reading, 1970 (r) Black Panther poster; Page 7 Afeni being led to courtroom, 1970; Page 9 Tupac, one year old, 1972; Page 10 Tupac with Mutulu, 1973; Page 11 Yafeu (Yaki) Fula and Tupac's cousin Jamaal Sheard; Page 12 (t) Tupac, Yafeu and Katari (Kastro), Riverside Park, NYC, 1980–1981, (b) Tupac and friends; Page 13 (t) Tupac and Quina Thornton, (b) Tupac with cousins; Page 15 (l) Afeni Shakur, Geronimo and Shaki Pratt, (r) Afeni, Shaki, and friends; Page 19 Tupac at Golden Gate Park, San Francisco, 1979; Page 20 (t) Tupac and Yafeu in Rye, NY, 1981, (b) Tupac, Yaasmyn and Yafeu Fula, Bronx, NY, 1978; Page 21 (t) Tupac and his sister Sekyiwa with Yafeu, San Francisco, CA, 1979, (b) Mai-Ling, Tupac and Sekyiwa, 1978; Page 22 Tupac, Sekyiwa and Jamal Sheard; Page 23 Tupac and Sekyiwa; Page 25 (clockwise from top left) Mutulu Shakur, "Legs" McNeil, Geronimo Pratt in San Quentin Prison, 1980; Pages 26–27 Tupac at Kwanza party with friends and family; Page 28 Tupac and family friends; Page 29 Tupac and Yafeu at Legal Services picnic, 1979; Page 35 Baltimore housing; Page 36 Afeni, Sekyiwa and friends in front of Baltimore home; Page 37 Sharonda Davila, Yafeu and Tupac, East Orange, NJ, 1984; Page 42 Tupac and cousins; Page 45 (l) Tupac and Jada Pinkett with classmates, (r) Tupac with classmates; Page 46 (l) Tupac, Kalil, Afeni and Kiana, March 10, 1986, (r) Tupac and Jonathan, March 10, 1986; Page 47 Tupac on his porch; Pages 48, 50, 51 Tupac and Jada; Page 53 (t) John Cole, (b) painting by John Cole; Page 55 Tupac's class at the Baltimore School for the Arts; Page 59 Tupac on Baltimore street circa 1988; Page 62 Marin County, CA; Page 68 (l) Yakisizwe, Tupac, Asinia, (r) Flava Flav signs autograph for Tupac; Page 72 (t) onstage in Japan, (b) onstage with Shock G; Pages 74-77 Digital Underground on tour; Page 84 (t) Michael Badalucco and Rony Clanton grill Tupac in *Juice*, (b) Bishop confronts Omar Epps's character in *Juice*; Page 87 Janet Jackson and Tupac in *Poetic Justice*; Pages 88-89 with friends and family; Page 91 (r) Tupac and Jasmine Guy; Page 92 Tupac and Jada; Page 94 (t) Tupac and Jada (b) Tupac and friends; Page 95-97 Tupac with friends and family; Page 99 as Birdie in *Above the Rim*; Page 100 onstage with Digital Underground; Pages 102-103 Tupac signs autographs during a break in filming *Above the Rim*; Page 104 (l) Tupac and friend, (r) Tupac at an airport; Page 105 (r) Treach, Tupac, and Easy E; Page 108 Tupac as Bishop in *Juice*; Page 109 Tupac on video shoot; Page 114 Tupac at his apartment in Marin City, CA; Page 118 Tupac at shooting range in Oakland, CA, 1992; Page 119 (r) Tupac and Yafeu (Kadafi) in Beverly Hills, CA 1993; Page 120 Tupac performing at the House of Blues, L.A.; Page 123 Tupac, Country, Syke, Mopreme, Scott Lesane and unidentified others; Page 124 (l) Tupac and Country (r) Tupac with Suge Knight; Page 128 Tupac, Scott (cousin), and "Man Man"; Pages 136-137 Tupac at L.A. Municipal Court, facing fifteen days jail sentence for assault and battery on film director Allan Hughes, 1994; Pages 143-144 Court drawings; Page 145 Tupac passes through courthouse metal detector; Page 146 Tupac being escortedto sentencing by Nation of Islam bodyguards; Page 148 Court drawing of sentencing; Page 152 Clinton Correctional prisoner ID; Page 157-159 incarcerated at Rikers Island; Page 174 (clockwise from left) with Jasmine Guy, with Dez, Big Syke, Keisha and friends, with Keisha and friends, and with Dez and her mother; Page 176 Keisha and Tupac on their wedding day; Page 178 Keisha in her apartment; Page 179 Keisha and Tupac; Page 199 Tupac, Suge Knight, Snoop Dogg as photographed for the New York Times Sunday Magazine cover; Page 201 Tupac in Hawaii, 1994; Page 202 (t) Tupac with friends and family, (b) Tupac with Yafeu (Kadafi) and Yafi; Page 203 (t) Sekyiwa, Afeni and Tupac, (b) Hammer, Tupac, Coolio, Snoop Dogg; Page 204 Tupac and nephew Malik; Page 209 (t) Tupac in the studio, (b) Dr. Dre, Johnny "J", Tupac, and Country in the studio; Page 210 Tupac with the "Outlawz" during the video shoot for "Hit 'em Up," 1996; Page 211 (t) Johnny "J" and his wife Capucine with Tupac, (b) Tupac and Dr. Dre; Page 215 Suge Knight and Tupac, "California Love" video shoot; Page 216 (t) Tupac, Johnny "J", Suge Knight, Hammer, (b) Karupt, Daz, Tupac, Johnny "J", and Snoop Dogg; Page 221 Tupac in dressing room, "Hit 'em Up" video shoot; Page 226 (t) Tupac, Shock G's brother Kent and Stretch, (b) Jamaal Sheard, Quina Thornton, and Tupac; Page 227 (t) Yafeu (Kadafi]) and Tupac; Page 228 (l) Afeni and Tupac, (r) Tupac at Free Geronimo Pratt rally; Page 232 (t) November 30, 1994, Times Square, NYC, (b) Tupac speaks at voter registration rally on August 15, 1996 in South Central, L.A.; Page 233 (t) Tupac in studio, (b) Tupac exiting the Digital Underground tour bus; Page 237 (clockwise from top left) with friend, on "How Do You Want It" video shoot, with Outlawz, with friends, with Big Syke and friends, Tupac and Afeni with friends, with friend, performing with the Outlawz at the 662 Club, Las Vegas, NV; Page 241 September 7, 1996, Las Vegas, Page 242 self portrait

Original Concept: Afeni Shakur

Editors: Jacob Hoye and Karolyn Ali

Photo Editor: Walter Einenkel

Design: Base

Rights and Clearances: Michelle Gurney and Andrea Glanz

Special thanks: Tupac Shakur

Additional thanks to: Ted Baer, Rick Barlowe, Vern Cambridge, Hillary Cohen, Geoff Cook, Rufus Cooper PKA Noble, Gloria Cox, Katari Cox PKA Kastro, Judith Curr, Donald David, Luke Dempsey, Linda Dingler, Barbara Ehrbar, Eric Farber, Henry Fayson, Yaasmyn Fula, Shock G., David Gale, Katy Garfield, Malcolm Greenidge PKA Edi, Wenonah Hoye, Natasha Jen, Sean Joelle-Johnson, Dimitri Jeurissen, Azon Juan, Spencer Galbreath, Dina LaPolt, Jamala Lesane, Dana Lixenberg, Kevin Lyons, Beth Matthews, TreMayne Maxie, Joey Molko, Vincent Sahli, Deeklah Polansky, Lisa Preston, George Pryce, Michael Rapaport, Jeri Rose, Lance Rusoff, Sekyiwa Shakur, Kim Shine, Lisa Silfen, Donald Silvey, Marcus Sommerville, Van Toffler, Dina Tyler, and Romall Watson.

Finally, profound gratitude to Afeni Shakur for her wisdom and inspiration and for providing the blueprint for Tupac's beautifully complex soul.

Photography courtesy of the following: Globe Photos, Inc.: pages 4, (l) 5, 9, (r) 104, (l) 105, 106, (r) 124, 136-137, 145, 146, (t) 232; Chi Modu: pages 131, 133, (b) 202, (t) 227; Mutulu Shakur: pages (r) 5, (b) 13, 116-117; Jada Pinkett Smith: pages 48, 92, top right 94; AP/WideWorld Photos: pages 7, (b) 232—Frank Weise; Amaru Entertainment: pages 10, 11, (b) 12, 15, (b) 21, 22, 25-29, 35, 46, 50, 51, 66, (l) 68, (t) 72, 89, 91, (b) 94, 95-97, (l) 104, 109, 112-114, 118, (l) 119, (l) 124, 129, 138, 174, 176, 178-179, (t) 202, (t) 203, 204, 209, (t) 210, 221, (b) 226, (b) 227, (t) 233; Johnny "J": pages (b) 209, (t) 211, 216; Gloria Cox: pages (t) 13, (r) 68 ; Yaasmyn Fula: pages (t) 12, 19, 20, 37, 59, (r) 119, 128, 152, 200-201, (b) 210, (t) 226, (l) 228 ; Sekyiwa Shakur: page (t) 21; Valli Barnes: pages 16, 17, 23, 38-41 (b) 42, (b) 211; Yearbook Archives: page 45; Adger Cowans: pages 84, 108; Victor Hall: pages 100, (b) 233; Shock G: pages (b) 72, bottom left 94; Shawn Mortensen: page 115; Baltimore School for the Arts: page 55; Kathy Crawford: page 65; John Barris: page 81; George Pryce: page 120; Randy Taylor: page (b) 203; Ant Dog: page 90; Big Syke: page 123; Treach: page (r) 105; Clinton Correctional Facility: page 154; New Line Cinema: pages 99, 102-103; Dana Lixenberg/Z Photographic: pages 157-159, 169, 182, 191-195; All court drawings by Shirley Shepard; Page 74 Digital Underground on tour (clockwise from top left) Victor Hall, DJ Fuze, Money B, Shock G, Shock G, Victor Hall; Page 75 Digital Underground on tour (clockwise from top left) DJ Fuze, DJ Fuze, Victor Hall; Page 76 Digital Underground (clockwise from top left) Victor Hall, Victor Hall, DJ Fuze, Victor Hall; Page 79 Digital Underground (clockwise from top left) DJ Fuze, Victor Hall, Victor Hall, Victor Hall, Victor Hall, Shock G; Page 237 (clockwise from top left) Amaru, Yaasmyn Fula, Asinia, Amaru, Amaru, Amaru, Yaasmyn Fula; Page 87 "Poetic Justice" © 1993 Columbia Pictures Industry Inc.; Page 199 Michael O'Neill/Corbis Outline; Page 215 Mojgan B. Azimi/Corbis Outline; Pages 224, 230, 239 Jeffery Newbury/Corbis Outline; Pages 231, 234 Danny Clinch/Corbis Outline; Page 241 Corjuni/Corbis Outline; Quote on page 82 *Juice* © Paramount Pictures; Portions of the text appear courtesy of Black Entertainment Television Inc.